CONNECT TO LEAD

Power Up Your Learning Network to Move Your School Forward

JACIE MASLYK

International Society for Technology in Education

PORTLAND, OREGON • ARLINGTON, VIRGINIA

Connect to Lead
Power Up Your Learning Network to Move Your School Forward
Jacie Maslyk

Senior Acquisitions Editor: *Valerie Witte*
Development and Copy Editor: *Linda Laflamme*
Proofreader: *Whitney Foster*
Indexer: *Valerie Haynes Perry*
Book Design and Production: *Jeff Puda*
Cover Design: *Edwin Ouellette*

Library of Congress Cataloging-in-Publication Data available

First Edition
ISBN: 9781564847782
Ebook version available
Printed in the United States of America
ISTE® is a registered trademark of the International Society for Technology in Education

About ISTE

The International Society for Technology in Education (ISTE) is a nonprofit organization that works with the global education community to accelerate the use of technology to solve tough problems and inspire innovation. Our worldwide network believes in the potential technology holds to transform teaching and learning.

ISTE sets a bold vision for education transformation through the ISTE Standards, a framework for students, educators, administrators, coaches and computer science educators to rethink education and create innovative learning environments. ISTE hosts the annual ISTE Conference & Expo, one of the world's most influential edtech events. The organization's professional learning offerings include online courses, professional networks, year-round academies, peer-reviewed journals and other publications. ISTE is also the leading publisher of books focused on technology in education. For more information or to become an ISTE member, visit iste.org. Subscribe to ISTE's YouTube channel and connect with ISTE on Twitter, Facebook and LinkedIn.

Related ISTE Titles

Building a K-12 STEM Lab: A Step-by-Step Guide for School Leaders and Tech Coaches
Deborah Kantor Nagler and Martha Osei-Yaw

To see all books available from ISTE, please visit iste.org/books.

About the Author

Credit: Theresa Glen Photography

As a connected educator and established school and district leader, Dr. Jacie Maslyk has served as a teacher, coach, principal, curriculum director, and assistant superintendent. She has presented at the state, national, and international level. A published author, Dr. Maslyk has written articles on a number of relevant topics, including STEM, instructional technology, leadership, and effective digital literacy strategies. She has published several professional education books, including *STEAM Makers: Fostering Creativity and Innovation in the Elementary Classroom* and *uNlocked: Opening a World of Creativity Within Your Students*. She has also written a chapter in the upcoming EduMatch Publishing book on makerspaces. An invited keynote speaker, Maslyk also consults with school districts looking to implement innovative practices in their schools.

Maslyk holds a bachelor's degree in elementary education and a master's degree in instructional leadership. She received a doctoral degree in curriculum and instruction from Indiana University of Pennsylvania in 2012 after conducting research on effective school leadership.

Website: **www.steam-makers.com**

Blog: *Creativity in the Making* at **Jacie.maslyk.blogspot.com**

Twitter: **@DrJacieMaslyk**

Instagram: **jaciemaslyk**

Acknowledgments

I want to thank several individuals who have been instrumental in making this book possible:

Thank you to all of the amazing educational leaders in the Pittsburgh region and the networks that you have fostered in order to bring creativity and innovation to our schools.

Thank you to all of the #Connect2Lead Educators who shared their stories about the importance of learning and growing as a connected educator.

Thank you to the entire team at ISTE, including Linda Laflamme, who provided ongoing support and feedback throughout this process; and especially Valerie Witte, who welcomed my ideas and encouraged me to write this book.

Thank you to my husband, my children, and my family for supporting my commitment to education and my love of writing.

Dedication

To Carrie, Cristine, Jane, and Michelle for supporting my crazy idea to start a connected network of learners. Thank you for pushing my thinking and serving as role models for what strong educational leaders can accomplish.

Contents

Introduction

A few years ago, I came to a crossroads as an educator. Maybe you have been there, too: a time in your career when you felt that something was missing. I was moving forward in my role as a building principal, and I enjoyed my job. I was just feeling a bit uninspired, as if I were on a personal pause. I needed to find a way to re-energize myself in my role as an educator.

Maybe you have found yourself at a similar intersection. Perhaps you're pondering changing grade levels or going back to school to study something new. It might be a moment that challenges you to decide if education is still the field for you. Everyone's pause at the crossroads may be different, but ultimately, it is a time when you choose one path or another.

My path led outward: I began going to more conferences and putting myself out there, connecting with other educators and building a personal network of support. Some of that support came in the form of new educator friends that I met at workshops or other local events. I expanded my circle of influence and started building relationships with educators that I could learn from—those that shared different perspectives from me. I felt as though I was broadening my views and being open to new ideas and experiences. My ability to connect was helping me to be a better leader.

During this time, I also joined Twitter. That may sound like an insignificant choice, but for me it was a game changer. Social media allowed me to feel connected to a global community of educators, reaching far beyond my former educational circle. I started reading blogs, listening to podcasts, and joining Twitter chats. As I expanded my network, I also expanded my views about my work as an educator. It's funny how being connected makes you think more deeply about other perspectives. It makes you more reflective, which prompted me to make the right turn at the crossroads, one that would help me to find new inspiration and momentum to propel me forward.

An entire community of educators, whether they knew it or not, was changing my outlook on education. This virtual learning network helped me to feel relevant again. The connections I made also gave me a newfound sense of power. That was just what I needed to feel recharged and ready to travel on a new path—one that would inspire me to try the latest technology tools and connect in different ways. This new path would allow me to look beyond my current circle of influence and discover so many opportunities for myself, my teachers, and my school. These connections helped me to expand learning for everyone in my school, moving us forward toward more relevant and engaging opportunities for all.

The world is moving at a rapid pace, with changing technologies and innovative career paths we can only imagine. Our schools are responsible for preparing students for an unknown future that will require expanded thinking, creative ideas, and complex problem solving. Our schools need to be spaces that will foster connected learning and innovative practices. With my renewed sense of purpose and powered up attitude, I was ready to take on the role of innovator and transform my leadership practices.

Power Up and Push Your Limits

Education needs innovators who are willing to push the limits to create schools that are inviting, collaborative, and innovative. This may be a new charge for some school leaders who have worked in the past as effective school managers. Leading innovation requires unconventional thinking and a passionate spirit on the part of school and district leadership. Powering up our leadership means that every part of the school community has a voice in this change. Learning networks are the key to powering up. They maximize learning for students and magnify collaboration and innovation for educators.

Learning networks can be physical or digital. They can focus on collaboration, effective instructional practices, or any number of educational topics. Learning networks can exist through social media tools or existing organizational structures, or these networks can be established and fostered by those who create them. Whatever type of learning network you become involved in, what matters most is that you take the necessary steps to be connected as an educator.

By emphasizing the importance of collaborative learning communities, school leaders can create systematic improvements in schools, districts, and regions. Leaders not only need to participate in global learning communities that stimulate innovation, creativity, and digital collaboration, they also need to model this proactive approach to powerful learning for their teachers. How can establishing learning networks around educational initiatives connect educators beyond the school walls?

With all that is on our plates as school and district leaders, we must each maintain our focus on our mission and vision for our own organization. While every school retains its own culture, initiatives, and identity, we are all moving our schools forward together to provide the best educational experience that we can for our students. Every school leader has his or her own style of leadership. This book is not to advocate for one style over another, but to say that every leader—from coaches to principals, directors to superintendents—needs to realize that moving a school or a district forward doesn't happen by you alone. It requires a strong team of educators, a supportive school community, collaborative parents and families, and eager students ready to learn.

Beyond this team of people, successful leaders are tapping into the power of learning networks. They realize that they can become stronger educators and leaders if they have the support and inspiration from others around them. Successful leaders understand the value of being connected to other educators through a learning network.

What's in This Book

Connect to Lead will illustrate not only the importance of professional learning, but also how to be a connected educator and leverage technology to learn within a collaborative network. Throughout the book you will find questions to prompt reflection for leaders and discussion for school teams and potential networks, as well as case studies of learning networks in action. These rich, real-world examples will provide insight into the benefits of learning networks, the many ways they can be formed, and the work that the power of a network can accomplish. As you read, be on the lookout for QR codes that, when scanned, will take you to useful resources referenced in the text. For instance, scanning the code on the left will take you to my website where you'll find digital copies of all the templates and checklists printed in the book. In addition, each chapter will provide inspiration and examples from school leaders and education innovators who are embracing change and creating momentum in their school districts, and end with "The Power of 3, 2, 1": three action steps you can take in response to the chapter content, two educators you should follow on Twitter, and one learning network you should learn more about. Be sure to use the QR code to visit my website often and check out videos and new content related to *Connect to Lead*.

Resources & Videos

This text will give you a new look at leadership and highlight the ISTE Standards for Education Leaders (International Society for Technology in Education [ISTE], 2018), focusing on the importance of a leader as:

Equity and Citizenship Advocate: Learn how networks help you provide resources to your school outside the constraints of your budget (Chapter 3).

Visionary Planner: Explore how to create a vision for collaboration in changing educational times (Chapter 1).

Empowering Leader: Meet connected leaders who provide an example of what empowering leadership looks like in action (Chapter 4).

Systems Designer: Develop an understanding of what it takes to create a collaborative network and design a system of connected support for your school (Chapter 2).

Connected Learner: Investigate pathways to foster connected learning for yourself, your teachers, your students, and your school community (Chapter 5).

Who This Book Is For

This book is for every K–12 administrator, curriculum director, technology coach, and teacher leader who wants to build relationships that will advance learning in their school. It's for educators who plan professional learning for others. It is for leaders, formal or informal, who have a vision for moving their schools and districts forward in a way that will have a positive impact on student learning.

It's also for educators who are at a crossroads and need to power up their own learning by connecting with others. Through these connections, we can serve as effective leaders, ensuring that our schools are future ready and poised to serve our students in a connected global society.

If you are ready to connect with others to leverage your leadership and move your school forward, this book will support you as you engage in powerful opportunities to advance learning. As you read, join others in this journey on Twitter by following the hashtag #Connect2Lead.

Let's connect!

Jacie

1

The Changing Educational Landscape

When I started in education, some twenty years ago, it was a pretty isolating profession. If I wanted to go into my classroom, close the door, and teach all day, I could do that. There was no call for collaboration or time to meet with colleagues. I could have kept my head down, stayed focused on my own students, and just kept on following my manual.

In fact, I did—until a colleague came into my room and asked me some hard questions about my reading instruction. He pushed me to think about the literacy development of my students. He encouraged me to look beyond the resources that I had been provided and consider instead what my students really needed. He introduced me to other teachers who were trying alternative ways to meet the needs of their struggling readers. Our common goal of helping our students succeed brought us together as a group.

While we created this informal connection through our own needs, our school was also embarking on a more formal initiative called *critical friends groups*. These groups were to foster dialogue among educators focused on effective instruction and student learning. Groups met monthly in classrooms and often shared student work. Sometimes we used specific protocols to focus on certain aspects of student development. It was a way to get different perspectives on our work and also connect with our colleagues. As a new teacher, I found the regular gatherings helpful, but my personal learning and professional development was limited to the other educators assigned to my group.

Fast forward twenty years: Our ability to connect and learn from others is now unlimited. Through the power of technology and the use of social media, we are no longer tied down to the other educators in our school districts, or even our states. We have the power to expand our personal and professional networks to include anyone across the globe. For example, my network now includes not only the educators in my local area, but also individuals both in and outside of education. With a tap of a button we can connect with STEM companies in Texas, school administrators in Virginia, makerspace gurus in London, and classroom teachers in Australia. At any moment, my learning can deepen and expand through the expertise of those who are within a network. This connectedness has helped me to become a stronger educator and a better leader. It has expanded my view of what effective teaching looks like and has fostered my interest in innovative learning opportunities for students. For my amazing colleague Kristen Nan, making connections with others was transformative, too:

> Being a connected educator has redefined my practice. There was a time when I thought the school day started and finished with me within my own four walls of thinking. Yes, a very closed-minded way of learning; yet, one that was instilled in me from the start and carried me through more years than I would like to admit. Breaking down the walls and connecting beyond my classroom has opened my mind to a variety of philosophies in teaching—ones that push me to be uncomfortable and challenge me to be better than the day before.

It can do the same for you.

Being connected makes us better. This is important because we are in the midst of an exciting time in education with schools adjusting their trajectories to ensure they are future ready. Educators are infusing creative programs and innovative teaching practices to move our schools forward. With a goal to push student thinking and advance teaching and learning, school leaders need to consider the possible strategies to leverage innovation in their schools.

Critical Shifts

What has occurred over the last several years to change the educational landscape? Foremost, three critical shifts have created opportunities for teachers and students to expand beyond what had traditionally been possible:

- Isolation to collaboration

- Consumption to creation

- Accountability to innovation

These shifts provide some focus toward the skills and dispositions that our students will need once they leave our schools to embrace their futures. Let's take a closer look at each of these shifts and how they are influencing our work as educators.

Isolation to Collaboration

Educators can no longer afford the mindset of continuing to do things the way they've always been done–alone in the classroom. This practice of isolation can be detrimental to the growth and development of not only our teachers, but also our students. The students in our schools aren't the same students from decades ago. Our practices need to shift in order to respond to their changing needs. We must seek out collaboration.

Our success as educators and as school leaders is all about relationships: the relationships we build with our students, with one another, and with the school community. It is this type of collaborative spirit that will advance our schools into the future. Through collaboration, teachers have the opportunity to share ideas and gain exposure to new practices. This moves us out of isolation and into a collaborative space where we are open to what those around us can offer. As leaders, this means that not only do we need to embrace collaboration in our roles, but that we also must set up the conditions for collaboration in our schools.

Collaboration can happen at different levels, both within the classroom and across your school. It can fuel new partnerships and solidify existing relationships. Although collaboration is natural for some, it may be new and more challenging for others. Table 1.1's "Collaboration Checklist" provides some questions for you to get the most out of your collaboration efforts at the school and district level, as well as the classroom level. The more "yes" answers you have, the more effective your collaborative efforts will be!

COLLABORATION CHECKLIST	Table 1.1

SCHOOL/DISTRICT LEVEL

○ Do you discuss the purpose for collaboration?

○ Are people clear about their role in collaborative groups?

○ Is there time allocated for collaboration between teams, grade levels, or departments?

○ Do educators engage in collaborative planning time?

○ Do educators brainstorm, create, and make decisions together?

○ Are shared resources created and used by collaborative teams?

○ Are teachers provided with opportunities to build skills and strategies to facilitate collaboration in the classroom with their students?

CLASSROOM LEVEL

○ Do teachers provide guidance and support so that students can effectively collaborate in the classroom?

○ Can students model effective communication skills?

○ Do students receive regular opportunities to collaborate with a variety of individuals?

○ Do students understand when to be a consumer and when to be a contributor in a collaborative group?

○ Do students know how to respond when collaboration is not effective?

What level of collaboration exists in your school or district? Do you have a powerful example of collaboration in action? Share a positive model of collaboration using #Connect2Lead.

Collaboration can occur in many ways. It can be developed through face-to-face interactions that you build with colleagues or sparked through the connections you make through your virtual networks. Whether you're reaching across your school hallway or state lines, technology tools can support your efforts. For example:

> **Trello** (**trello.com**) (Figure 1.1). Designed for creating and tracking projects, Trello enables team members to share files, ideas, and notes. You can work through the browser-based interface or an app on your iOS or Android mobile device.

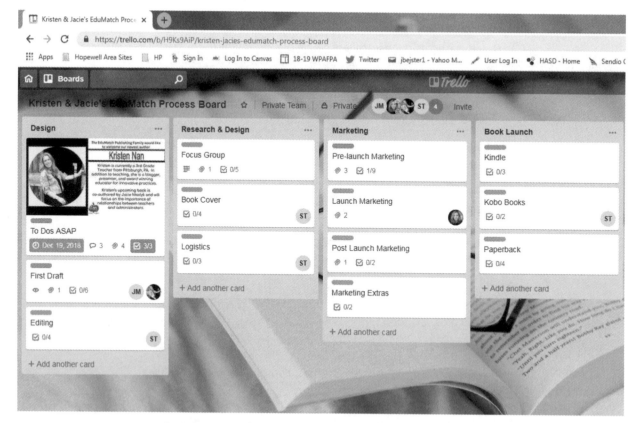

Figure 1.1 Trello helps you track your collaborative projects.

Slack (**slack.com**) (Figure 1.2). This collaborative hub can house projects for you and your team. Creating different channels, you can streamline work with those in your network using the iOS, Android, or web-based version.

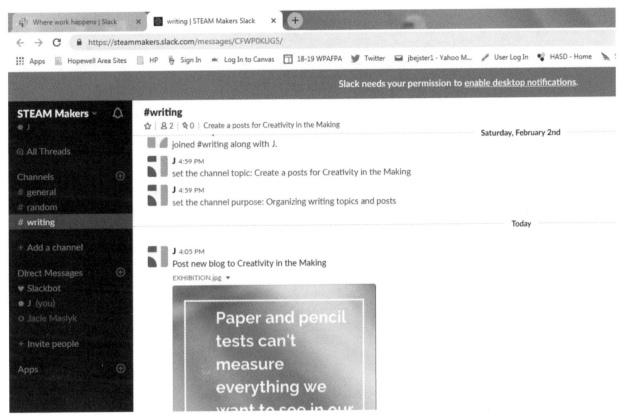

Figure 1.2 Slack helps you and your network work together.

Mural (**mural.co**) (Figure 1.3). Not just for designers, this visual collaboration tool allows teams to connect ideas, images, and videos on a shared whiteboard. Mural is cloud-based and can be used with any device.

These and other tools will be discussed throughout the book for those of you who are looking to use technology to accelerate your learning and move your schools forward in innovative ways.

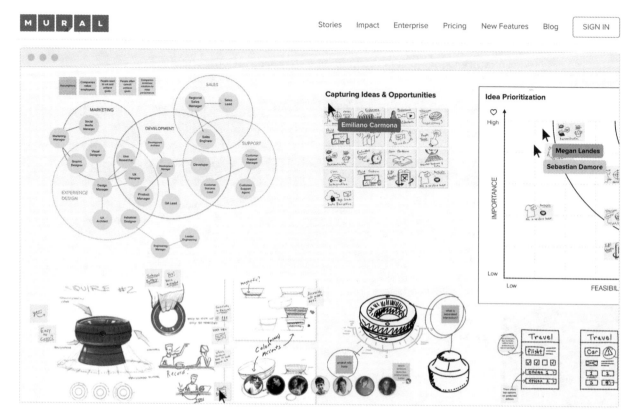

Figure 1.3 Mural acts as a cloud-based whiteboard.

Consumption to Creation

The shift from isolation to collaboration has also changed what is happening within our classrooms. With a focus on student-driven learning, we no longer hold all of the knowledge as educators. Our students no longer wait for us to deliver new information to them; instead they are constantly connecting with others and constructing new knowledge of their own. This generation of learners is no longer satisfied with merely consuming information, and forward-thinking school leaders are encouraging students to shift from being consumers to creators. As reflected in the ISTE Standards for both Educators and Students, the need for creativity and innovation is stronger than ever. What better way for students to show what they know than by designing and creating something that captures that learning!

Access to technology is accelerating our students' ability to create. When students are equipped with devices to access creative apps and tech tools to support engineering, robotics, and coding, their imaginations soar. This is a stark contrast to classrooms that focus on consumption. Here are a few tips for facilitating creation as opposed to consumption in your school:

- Encourage teachers to plan at least one learning activity each month (more or less depending on the strengths and needs of your team).

- Celebrate student creation in public ways, such as hosting a student showcase of science projects, writing, art, performances, and so on.

- Plan evening events that engage students and families in hands-on creation.

- Spread good news about student creation through a district social media page, electronic newsletter, or website.

When students create, they feel empowered over their own learning. Here are some helpful ideas for free tools to promote student creation in the classroom:

- Inspire writing and create books using **Storybird** (**storybird.com**).

- Organize images and text in the **Paper** app (**wetransfer.com/products**) to design a virtual scrapbook.

- Try **ThingLink** (**thinglink.com**) to make interactive videos and images.

- Use **PowToon** (**powtoon.com**) to make animations.

- Try a screencasting tool, like **Screencast-O-Matic** (**screencast-o-matic.com**), to create recordings of your on-computer actions or the **TouchCast Studio** (**touchcast.com/studio**) app, which allows you to create broadcasts straight from your iOS device.

- Design posters and infographics with **Canva** (**canva.com**).

These are just a few examples of how you can use technology to shift from consumption to creation. Throughout the book's stories and case studies, other educators and leaders will share their favorite technology tools for engaging learners.

Accountability to Innovation

The shift from accountability to innovation does not mean that accountability for student growth is no longer a factor, but rather that we are finally seeing a student's ability to think critically and innovate as valued. Schools are shifting from what seemed like a sole focus on test scores toward a more well-rounded portrait of student learning. We are looking beyond what a test score can show us and considering the talents, interests, and creative abilities of our students; stepping away from the traditional mindset toward a more flexible mindset. This flexibility is evident through the changing learning spaces in our schools, as well as our gradual, but much needed, move away from standardized testing, standardized curricula, and standardized instruction to student-centered, personalized learning options for students and for teachers.

With an emphasis on creation and innovation, as opposed to consumption, our students are being exposed to more opportunities than ever before to design, engineer, and invent. As we fuel their creative minds, we are seeing amazing results from students as they develop new apps, build complex video games, and create multimedia presentations. This shift is reflective of what is happening in our economy as innovative start-up companies grow out of new ideas and collaborative projects. Our students have the ability to innovate and create new things that might just be the next big thing.

According to corporate speaker and author Paul Sloane, "Creativity is thinking of something new. Innovation is implementing something new." Many have embraced the term *innovation* in education, as it signals changes from the status quo to more robust and relevant educational opportunities for our students. It ushered us into the 21st century and pushes us to think critically about the changes that will be necessary for our students to succeed in 2020, 2030, and beyond. With a renewed sense of enthusiasm, we are rethinking teaching and learning in a way that calls on every educational stakeholder to consider the possibilities for teaching and learning in their school communities. These shifts don't come without some challenges.

Challenges and Change

With these three educational shifts come change. Change can be a challenge, even scary, for educators, because it requires them to do something that isn't like their own learning experience. There has never been a time in education where the educational experiences of the teachers were so vastly different from the lives and habits of current students—think about that.

When these shifts impact you, you may feel uncomfortable at times. There will be things that you won't have experience with, but that is the beauty of a learning network. In a network, you have a community there to support you as you change the status quo. You can surround yourself with people you are comfortable with, or who might already have experience with whatever is new to you. Networks make you feel like you are not alone. It is this collective pushing forward for change that makes our instruction better. It improves learning environments for students. It takes teaching and learning on a new path that is invigorating.

As school leaders, we need to recognize that change may be difficult and present a variety of challenges to school leadership. Instead, make change an amazing journey as students and teachers become re-engaged in learning. When teachers are struggling, school leaders need to roll up their sleeves, move in beside the teacher, and help them figure it out. If they want to try something new, help them find the resources. We can leverage the technologies at our fingertips to advance professional learning by creating instructional or inspirational videos. We can connect teachers with experts and other educators who can support them as they're trying to engage students in new kinds of learning experiences. In addition, we need to consider the ways that the skills of the digital age are evident in our daily work, which includes our professional learning. If we want to see these skills in action in our classrooms, we need to start by preparing our teachers for the kind of instructional approaches that will support their development.

Right Now Skills

Whether you call them the skills of the digital age or the Four Cs, they are the skills that our students need to build *right now* to navigate complex problems. When we design our instruction to promote these skills, we are preparing our students for present and future challenges while transforming learning from a passive, compliant model to one that is active and engaging for students. These "Right Now Skills" became popularized by the Partnership for 21st Century Learning Framework and include:

- Creativity
- Critical thinking
- Communication
- Collaboration

All four provide a learner-centered approach to the classroom. They are skills that we can't "do" to our students; they have to be developed and embraced by the students themselves. When your students activate their creativity in the classroom, it is their chance to express themselves in interesting and imaginative ways. When we design lessons that prompt critical thinking, our students can tap into strategies that require complex problem solving. Communication in the classroom may be a part of participating in group work and sharing ideas, but more importantly, student communication can come in the form of student voice being used as a means of projecting opinions, debating arguments, and reaching out to others through face-to-face interactions or with the use of virtual tools. The importance of communication often lends itself to the development of collaboration, which is at the heart of this book. Our ability to connect with others and develop collaboration skills will benefit both our students and our teachers.

Our students need these skills *right now*, as do our teachers. Building Right Now Skills can be advanced through relevant instructional strategies like STEM, STEAM, and maker education.

STEM and STEAM

Through STEM and STEAM initiatives, educators are moving beyond the learning silos of isolated subject areas and moving toward a more integrated approach that more closely mirrors the work that students will engage in once they leave our schools. STEM education represents an opportunity for students to engage in hands-on learning that incorporates some aspect of science, technology, engineering, or math. STEAM education incorporates art, music, literature, or history into the mix, as well. This kind of learning takes the focus off of the classroom teacher and enables students to engage in challenges and solve complex problems using the skills that they have learned in each content area.

#Connect2Lead Educator: Justin Aglio

An educational leader on the cutting edge, Dr. Justin Aglio (@JustinAglio) is a forward-thinking educator who is not only a true Systems Designer (ISTE Standards for Education Leaders. 2018), but is also leading his district in the right direction. With his district leadership team, he has established partnerships with business, industry, and other education leaders to support the strategic and innovative vision for his school district and ensure the resources for supporting the effective use of technology for learning are accessible to students and teachers. When other schools were starting STEM programs, his district was already providing robotics instruction for students and coding courses for teachers. When some schools were considering how to transform their outdated computer labs, Justin was establishing partnerships with funders and local universities to establish a virtual reality lab in his district's high school. He reached out to his network, leveraging the relationships that he developed with organizations that could advance learning for his students. As schools worked to design makerspaces in their libraries and classrooms, Justin worked with the district administrative team to design a new elementary school that would house multiple innovative learning spaces. Two of those unique spaces were established through business partnerships with Lego and Minecraft. His ability to call on those within his learning network for the betterment of his teachers and the students in his school district sets him apart as a connected leader making a difference.

Making and Makerspaces

Have you ever walked into a makerspace in the midst of a student work session? It's impossible not to feel the creative buzz. Encompassing building, designing, hacking, and constructing, making is the creative intersection of art, science, technology, and design that results in the innovative thinking and problem solving of our students. It is a way to pull every student into the learning, as making is an inclusive strategy that allows every student to find their strength.

Maker learning has triggered the development of new learning spaces in classrooms, libraries, and communities. These spaces, equipped with maker materials from hand tools to 3-D printers, provide unlimited opportunities for students entering the space with an interest in creation This is not the space for consumption. In a makerspace, there is a sense of community where learners have gathered to connect with one another. Every learner comes ready for the chance to build and thrive.

Making creates a community for those who gather to share new knowledge and skills with their fellow makers. There is often a feeling of excitement and wonder as students are talking and building. Essentially, these young makers are creating their own network of learners, as they gather and share ideas. It is this type of learning that often brings people together around a common interest, much like the professional learning networks that we have as educators.

Connect to Innovate, Connect to Lead

School leaders need to be prepared for the impact that these critical shifts may have on their schools. The emergence of STEM, STEAM, and maker learning, for instance, may affect the way that teachers are providing instruction in the classroom and the way we design learning spaces to support students. The critical shifts from consumption to creation, and accountability to innovation, may also change curriculum, change the way that we map out learning paths, and even lead to changes in the way that we assess student learning.

If our goal within this new educational landscape is to create connections that will leverage learning for our teachers and students, then we need to shift the way we are approaching professional learning. We can no longer afford to provide solely large group in-service training sessions that were designed for a one-size-fits-all approach. Instead, educators need to carefully craft learning opportunities and networks that offer a variety of pathways to personal and professional growth.

Notice that I said *educators*, not just leaders. This isn't just a call to the bosses at the top or district leaders to lead change in our schools. Advancing our collective learning means that every part of the school community has a voice in this change. In order to truly prepare our young people for college, career, or whatever other path they may choose, we need to innovate at *all* levels. This means that we need our students to take the lead, not just our school administrators. It means that we need our teachers to feel empowered to lead change in their classrooms and in their schools. We need to flatten the hierarchy so that central office teams are not the only ones making important decisions about the future of education. This change can occur through learning networks that maximize learning for students and magnify collaboration and innovation for educators.

Not only can this change maximize learning, it helps meet the ISTE Standards for Education Leaders in several ways. This change reflects the need for all educators to become Connected Learners (ISTE, 2018), using technology tools to leverage our own learning, and also the learning of our students. With an increased emphasis on collaboration, we can use our connections to design our schools as interconnected systems to support learning at all levels. This is a call for all educators to rethink their practices and power up their ability to lead their school into the future.

The following chapters will provide you with some ideas for navigating the relevant shifts happening in education, as well as reflections from connected leaders about their learning networks.

The POWER of 3, 2, 1

3 Steps to Take

1. Identify one educational shift that is impacting your school. Write down possible **opportunities** you can take action on in response to that shift.

2. In what ways are you **welcoming** collaboration in your school or district? If collaboration is not embedded in your practice, what is one question from the "Collaboration Checklist" (Table 1.1) that you can focus on this week?

3. As you dig deeper into the topic of professional learning and the networks that support this work, what is one area that you can enhance to provide more **engaging** experiences in your role?

2 Educators to Follow on Social Media

Want to keep up to date on the shifts in education? Follow **Rachelle Dene Poth** (**@Rdene915**)! She is a connected educator working at the intersection of technology, STEAM, augmented reality, virtual reality, and foreign language. She engages in a number of Twitter chats and Voxer groups, actively pursuing new knowledge and sharing ideas with others. She leads the weekly #formativechat and is a part of the 4 O'Clock Faculty PLN. She is also the president of the ISTE Teacher Education Network #ISTETEN. Establishing partnerships to support the vision of her school district, Rachelle is a Systems Designer (ISTE, 2018) using her relationships and knowledge to maximize student learning.

Another connected educator leading change in her county is **Dr. Heather Kaiser** (**@technotchr**). As a gifted support specialist in the Cumberland County School District in Fayetteville, North Carolina, Heather has taken the lead in bringing the maker movement to her county. She hosts her district Twitter chat and also facilitates virtual meetings for her large district via Vidyo (**vidyo.com**), during which teachers can discuss maker tools and innovative programs throughout their schools. Demonstrating what it means to be a Learner (ISTE Standards for Educators, 2017), Heather continually looks to improve her practice, learning from and with others. She openly explores new ways to leverage technology to improve student learning.

1 Learning Network You Should Read More About

ISTE Connect

Check out **ISTE Connect** (**connect.iste.org/community/learningnetworks**) to learn about all of the online professional communities that can help you to power up your learning. The communities include interest areas, such as:

- Arts and technology
- Digital citizenship
- Digital storytelling
- Edtech coaches
- Games and simulations
- Inclusive learning
- Interactive video conferencing
- Librarians
- Mobile learning
- STEM
- Technology coordinators
- Computer science

- Digital equity
- Early learning
- Education leaders
- Global collaboration
- Independent and international schools
- Learning spaces
- Literacy
- Online learning
- Teacher education
- Virtual environments

Connecting to Standards

ISTE STANDARD FOR EDUCATION LEADERS

4. Systems Designer.

Leaders build teams and systems to implement, sustain and continually improve the use of technology to support learning. Education leaders:

4a Lead teams to collaboratively establish robust infrastructure and systems needed to implement the strategic plan.

4b Ensure that resources for supporting the effective use of technology for learning are sufficient and scalable to meet future demand.

4c Protect privacy and security by ensuring that students and staff observe effective privacy and data management policies.

4d Establish partnerships that support the strategic vision, achieve learning priorities and improve operations.

Continuous improvement through effective professional learning can be enhanced through a learning network.

ISTE STANDARD FOR EDUCATORS

1. Learner.

Educators continually improve their practice by learning from and with others and exploring proven and promising practices that leverage technology to improve student learning.

Ongoing personal learning and exploration of promising practices as educators leads to improved learning for students.

Powering Up Your Learning Network

How many times have you been corralled (or corralled everyone) into an auditorium or large group instruction space to prepare for a full day of professional development? Attendees reluctantly trudge in, disengaged before the day even begins. We have all spent time passively sitting in uncomfortable seats listening to some speaker espouse their knowledge to us. Whether at a session of state-mandated training on CPR or on some new district procedure, we know what it is like to spend the day on topics that are not relevant to improving our teaching practice. Professional development doesn't have to be this way.

We all yearn for a *personalized* approach to professional learning that allows us to pursue our interests and tailor our learning toward topics that are relevant to our daily work. If we take the time to consider how we can create a positive impact on the educators that we serve, professional development options can be powerful and empowering.

Michelle Miller, superintendent of Hopewell Area School District in Pennsylvania, understands the importance of powering up your learning network to engage learners at all levels, explaining, "Connection is the heart of school success. Engagement and growth are inevitable when teachers connect to students, educators network with other educators, and school leaders embrace relationships with educational and business leaders" (personal communication, 2019). The power of relationships like these allow schools and districts to thrive.

Mirroring the shifts happening in education with new technology and new instructional approaches, professional learning, too, is expanding beyond traditional "sit and get" to more engaging, connected, learner-driven opportunities. As you'll discover in this chapter, encouraging personal networks for educators is one key to transforming the professional learning plan in your school. I'll provide a framework for not only powering up your leadership, but also igniting a spark that your professional learning has been missing.

When we tap into strategies to increase our connectivity with others, the outcomes can be powerful for teachers and leaders alike. This happens within our buildings, but can be magnified when we extend our reach beyond our own walls and build relationships with others, expanding our educational community.

PLC, PLF, PLE—Oh My!

Over the last thirty years, the idea of professional educators gathering together has emerged as an effective practice, even more so in the last ten years as technology has advanced our ability to connect beyond traditional boundaries. To build a collaborative culture and support collegial relationships, schools and districts have created a variety of structures to support reflective practices through professional learning models.

Whether you participate in a *professional learning community* (PLC), grow in a *personal learning network* (PLN), or enjoy the support of a *professional learning family* (PLF), you understand the potential benefits of crowdsourcing your professional development. In her *Shift eLearning* blog post "What Are Personal Learning Networks" (2016), Karla Gutierrez pointed out that learning networks aren't new, but the power of technology has changed our ability to connect with others and expand our reach. To reflect that increased reach, she recommended the term *PLE* (*personal learning environment*), which encompasses both physical and digital networks of support. No matter the terminology, the idea behind it remains the same: We can grow stronger through our connectedness with other innovative educators.

Because we don't have quite enough acronyms surrounding this topic of connected learning in a collaborative group, let's add another: Emerging in recent years, the term *community of practice* (*CoP*) refers to a group of people who come together with a tighter focus. They may share a common passion, concern, or interest. Their goal is to learn and grow through regular interactions and communication within the community. These CoPs are meant to be an ongoing and collaborative way to discuss pertinent educational issues and grapple with ideas surrounding it.

A networked approach to learning provides some things that traditional professional learning cannot. As a connected educator within a learning network, you can personalize your learning pathway. If you develop an interest in a literacy topic, for example, you can reach out to the network and pursue it, finding ready-to-use strategies for your classroom. If a team within the network wants to learn more about maximizing the use of a new app, simply connect with your network and seek out the expertise of those around you. You don't get this when you work in isolation. Your needs and the needs of your network adjust in response to the group. It is essentially the mindset that we are better together. Consider a few more potential benefits:

- Pathway to develop yourself professionally

- Stay up to date

- Learn from different perspectives

- Share materials and resources

- Offer and receive advice

- On demand learning, there when you need it

In "Technology in the Classroom: The Connected Teacher" (n.d.), Jordan Catapano discussed the value of learning networks and why every educator needs one. He explained that when you create your own personal network, you are surrounding yourself with educators that will help make you a better teacher, a better leader, just better overall. The relationships that you build can be accessed when you need them, a benefit which is even more enhanced through the use of technology.

By connecting with others in your network through social media or other digital age avenues, you move beyond the "traditional routes" for learning and build skills that are beyond what has traditionally been expected. In the past, for example, you could gain this sense of support through a college course or a cohort program at a university. These models provided a sense of camaraderie as a group of individuals moved through a paced program together. This is still a great way to connect with others and develop professional relationships, but if we are to continue to grow, we need ways to access our network whether we are enrolled in courses or not. The idea of a learning network shouldn't be limited to a specific time or location, but be more of an ongoing support system that will change and grow as much as its members do.

Social media can be used to extend the learning beyond one conversation and connect learners across the globe. By developing professional relationships digitally, the collaboration can be immediate. Educators can post blogs, questions, pictures, and experiences and get quick feedback from their network. As a connected educator, it is this type of communication that can transform your practices. The ability to tap into the expertise from your network at the touch of a button is a game changer!

What Exactly Is a Learning Network?

For the purpose of this text, a *learning network* is a group of individuals who find strength in new knowledge, and inspiration and support from the collective ideas of others. A network can be a physical group that gathers within your building discussing relevant topics and learning together. A network can also be a group that you've never even met: a group of educators who connect virtually and provide similar supports and ideas. It is a way for educators to link with others who may provide common insight or profound new ideas. As Randy Ziegenfuss, superintendent of Pennsylvania's Salisbury Township School District explained,

> As educators, we each have tacit knowledge related to our practice. Through the power of networks, this knowledge is uncovered when we add our knowledge to the network, access the knowledge of others within the network, and together create new knowledge to solve common challenges of practice. In a rapidly shifting world and domain of education, it is critical that we participate in networks. It is one of the most powerful means we have to keep learning together to solve the problems of transforming teaching and learning. (personal communication, 2019)

With the advancement of technology, virtual networks are more and more common, but there is still a primal need to have face-to-face conversations with our networks.

Throughout this book, you will read examples of both: thriving face-to-face networks of innovators who come together in an empowering professional learning experience and digital learning networks of members who gain strength from those they connect with through social media.

In her book *Digital Citizenship in Action,* Kristen Mattson described a "participatory citizenship approach" (2017, p. 35), which highlighted digital citizens as consumers and contributors. Learning networks offer opportunities for these roles, as well, as some members lead while others listen. Some collect while others create. Some strategize while others investigate. In a "Personal Learning Networks for Educators: 10 Tips" (2012), Mark Wagner further broke down the roles within a learning network to:

- Connect
- Converse
- Contribute
- Request

Sometimes an individual may request and consume ideas and information from a network because that is what they need to learn and grow, but at another time that same individual may be a lead contributor.

Catapano (n.d.) also discussed the idea of leadership with respect to the facilitation of the learning network: A network approach allows the members of the group to adjust course and make choices about their learning. Traditional models would dictate where, when, and what you would learn—and often with who. Learning networks foster cross-group collaboration in whatever way works for the individuals. It's not led by a professor or a formal leader, but rather led by those who make up the network.

At the same time, learning networks are not haphazard; they are intentional. When we connect as a network, we have a purpose of learning and gaining information from others. It is a way for us to engage in collaboration that is sustained over time, not the "one and done" that often occurs with traditional professional development models. No matter what you may call the group you learn with, it is important to have a group.

The opportunity to be supported by a learning network may be something you take for granted. Maybe you have underestimated the value of such a group. Maybe you haven't experienced personalized learning. As school leaders, we are so busy with all that encompasses our daily work that perhaps we don't have the chance to recognize how a learning network could enhance our work. I would argue that you can't take the chance *not* to engage with your learning group. In the fast-paced world that we live in, new ideas, and especially new technologies, are changing rapidly. Connected leaders recognize the importance of staying relevant and making an impact on the teachers they serve. The lack of a connected learning network may be the difference between staying relevant and falling behind.

Proof Networks Work

Learning networks can provide benefits to you and the educators in your schools, as a growing body of research supports. At the Center for Collective Intelligence at the Massachusetts Institute of Technology (MIT) Sloan School of Management, researcher Peter Gloor (2017) is leading a project called Collaborative Innovation Networks (COIN), which explores the power of learning networks. Through his research, Gloor found that within an innovative network there will be visionaries, collaborators, and communicators. Not only do these characteristics connect with the Right Now Skills discussed in Chapter 1, but also with the ISTE Standards for Education Leaders, as you'll see in upcoming chapters. The idea behind Gloor's research is that leaders can employ principles of creative collaboration, knowledge sharing, and social networking to encourage educators to be more creative, productive, and efficient. Creating access and connectivity in education also addresses an important issue around equity, which will be discussed in the next chapter.

POWER UP Framework

As we move away from traditional methods of learning in the classroom, we must also move away from traditional methods of professional learning toward a more personalized, collaborative model. Some districts offer innovative days full of hands-on learning and opportunities to collaborate and plan new learning with our colleagues, for instance. The POWER UP Framework (Figure 2.1) is one way to ensure that you are responding to educational shifts in a way that translates to meaningful professional learning and collaboration for your teachers. It focuses on the power of being connected and using a learning network, whether physical or digital, to advance learning.

Powering up our leadership means that, as school and district leaders, we develop relationships and create partnerships that will leverage learning for our students, as well as for our teachers. As school leaders, we are on a mission to move our schools forward, creating endless opportunities for students with a focus on the future. Part of that mission means taking a leadership stance that empowers our teachers to be innovative and connected both in and out of school. When we power up our leadership, it means that we are incorporating seven key ideas that can support innovative practices, meaningful professional learning, and connected networks of learners. Activating these ideas empowers teachers and creates an environment that fosters innovation. The seven ideas that demonstrate the need for leadership are:

- **P**ersonalized
- **O**pportunities
- **W**elcoming
- **E**ngaging
- **R**elationships
- **U**nconventional
- **P**artnerships

POWER UP Leadership

Personalized
Opportunities
Welcoming
Engaging
Relationships

Unconventional
Partnerships

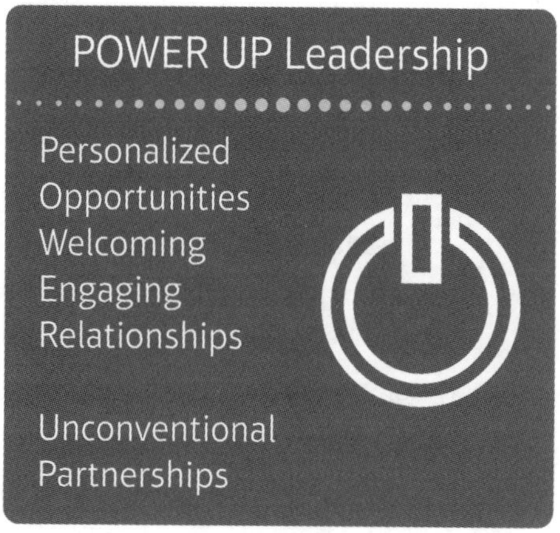

Figure 2.1 The POWER UP Framework can serve as a guide on your journey to move your school forward toward collaborative, innovative professional learning.

Let's take a closer look at each of these key ideas.

Personalized

Learning is personal for students and for educators. Every connected educator chooses a personalized path to learning. They make decisions about their personal and professional growth, which allows them to create connections within their learning network. When leaders have the ability to offer personalized options to their team, educators activate their voice and choice in the process. When we tap into personalization, professional learning might be tailored to meet individual needs, modes of learning may be different, and pathways to success may be designed for every learner.

Opportunities

As leaders, we need to always be on the lookout for opportunities to move our schools forward. This happens in the way that we share our story with others. It happens in the way we design professional learning for our teachers. It's how we find grants to fund projects and in the way we seek out opportunities to improve the educational system that we work in. How do powered up leaders find opportunities?

Welcoming

When we power up our leadership, we are choosing to take an approach that is welcoming and inclusive for all. It means that we welcome all learners within our schools, but also welcome parents and community members as a part of our learning network. It means that we foster all teachers as teacher leaders and build their ability to welcome others. When we are welcoming, we think about those who are on the fringe and design strategies that will intentionally bring them into the fold.

Engaging

Teaching and learning is not a passive act. It is not something that you do or that is done to you, but rather it is a practice that we must fully engage in. School leaders need to take steps to ensure that all aspects of the school are engaging—the environment, the curriculum, the technology. We also need to actively engage everyone in learning, especially our students, but also our teachers. When we engage teachers in professional learning, we help them to grow and expand their knowledge. When we engage teachers beyond their classroom by connecting them with a supportive network of learning, engagement deepens.

Relationships

Every successful educator knows that it is all about relationships: the relationships with your students, with parents, with the community, and with other educators. We build relationships with those in our schools as we connect with them daily through face-to-face conversations. We build relationships globally, through the power of technology. We foster relationships with other organizations beyond our schools through the partnerships that we create and the network that we choose to build. Relationships are like construction when you think about it. We lay the foundation. We build it brick by brick, making adjustments as we go to ensure stability. We use the tools and resources around us to keep our structure supported and strong, just as we do with our relationships. Without this, we won't be successful as individuals and certainly not as school leaders.

Unconventional

At times, our approach to leadership may be a little unconventional. We may choose a unique approach to professional learning or propose a project that seems a little off the beaten path at first; sometimes we need to do that. Thinking outside the box has become a part of education in the 21st century. We are looking for different ways to meet the needs of the learners around us, and, in this age of innovation, it is often the unconventional solutions that solve complex problems. As we push our students to think in this way, we must also support our teachers. Unconventional thinking on the part of school leaders may mean expanding your network to include unusual partnerships or unique learning opportunities. Unexpected strategies and non-traditional approaches to teaching and learning might be just what your school needs.

Partnerships

Part of our role as educators is to make sure that students leave our schools ready for college and careers. We must provide them with a variety of pathways that will take them out into an unknown world with unknown possibilities. How do we possibly prepare for this? One way is by capitalizing on the partnerships, local and global, that can leverage new learning for our students and teachers. Finding potential partnerships, building and maintaining these relationships, and using them to advance learning is now a part of school leadership. We can no longer remain managers of our schools; we need to be stewards of innovative teaching and learning.

Combined Power

The strategies within the POWER UP Framework are effective when applied individually, but there is even more power when school leaders are able to combine all of these together and create positive school change. As we all push to provide cutting edge learning in our schools, let's equip ourselves with the tools needed to design meaningful, connected learning and power up our leadership to form learning networks that can advance innovation.

POWER UP Case Study:
Beaver Area School District

The Beaver Area School District offers Individualized Professional Development Plans (IPDP), in which the educators choose what, where, and when they will learn. The district maintains days throughout the school year in which teachers can obtain their required professional development hours. During these days, there is a mix of teacher-led and district-facilitated learning sessions. Teachers don't have to attend these, though, especially if they can find another option that will better meet their needs and fully *engage* them in learning. The local museum is hosting a workshop? Teachers can attend. The community college is offering a session on community *partnerships*? Teams can attend this instead. At the end of the school year, teachers who still need professional development hours have the chance to attend a week of sessions on a variety of topics, including augmented and virtual reality, robotics, and even Google certification. Those who have acquired all their hours are done for the summer. This flexible approach to *personalized* professional learning provides teachers with unlimited *opportunities* to continue their professional growth.

Powerful Professional Learning

Learning networks can serve as a pathway to professional development (PD). Our networks can facilitate PD in both informal and formal ways—from the small nuggets of expertise that we gain from colleagues within a Twitter chat to more in-depth strategies that we learn from a blog. We can also design powerful learning experiences that members of our learning network can engage in through collaborative opportunities within our school communities. Learning networks, like some that you will learn about in this book, begin with the idea of shared, collaborative professional development and connect with educators in other districts, counties, or regions. We can blur the lines between our schools and districts and take a more collaborative approach to the way we learn together. This may be an unconventional approach, but that is one reason why the POWER UP Framework can benefit your leadership practice.

The POWER UP strategies can also be used in the professional development that you design in your own schools. You can take the ideas behind the benefits of a learning network and begin to build those same structures within your building. From the way you create smaller learning communities to the way you promote the Four Cs in your planning, you can create learning opportunities that can reap the same benefits.

Take a minute to evaluate the professional learning that you are offering to your teachers. It is important to maximize the time we have with our teachers and provide learning that offers connections and the building of relationships that can impact classroom instruction. Reflect on the questions in Table 2.1's "Professional Development Checklist" to determine if the professional development opportunities in your school or district are preparing teachers to develop future-ready skills.

If the professional learning in your district is checking lots of items off the list, share your best practices using #Connect2Lead. Our community of educators will benefit from your expertise. If you aren't able to agree that the components listed in Table 2.1 are a part of the learning that you offer to your educators, then how can you expect them to provide those chances for students? When implemented, these strategies empower your teachers and shift professional learning to an approach that is more collaborative, creative, and innovative.

This can take different forms within your PD plans. Are you looking to make things more collaborative? Try a group design challenge or a scavenger hunt to bring teachers together. Want them to explore new materials or learning tools? Provide an "innovation lounge" or other open space during your next professional development day. This will provide teachers with a low-pressure way to tinker with new resources and help them feel comfortable to implement the tools in a way that works for them. This setup also creates a low-stress environment where teachers can ask questions and work with their peers.

Want something more personalized? Some teachers might want the option to learn virtually through a Moodle site (**moodle.org**) or Schoology (**schoology.com**).You can create content for teachers (or better yet, they can create it for one another) designing learning modules or discussion groups that can push thinking and generate new knowledge. These online platforms allow teachers to move at their own pace and access the information that will best serve their needs and the needs of their students. Other sites like Hoonuit (**hoonuit.com**) and Participate (**participate.com**)

PROFESSIONAL DEVELOPMENT CHECKLIST   Table 2.1

DOES YOUR PD...

○ Engage teachers in collaborative challenges?

○ Offer creative choices in learning tasks?

○ Design learning opportunities that foster teacher critical thinking?

○ Create opportunities for teachers to engage in communication?

○ Embed personal reflection on digital age skills and dispositions?

○ Incorporate hands-on learning?

○ Offer time and space to explore new materials?

○ Provide new technologies for self-paced learning?

○ Extend opportunities for teachers to connect with others?

○ Include virtual learning options?

offer pre-made content on relevant topics like social-emotional learning, augmented reality, or project-based learning. Professional development can take many different forms. As we move toward more personalized options, those forms are going to continue to expand (Figure 2.2).

One way that districts are personalizing professional learning for teachers is through *micro-credentialing*: competency-based, on-demand learning opportunities. These certifications can be earned by teachers through both in-district designed formats, as well as out-of-district platforms. For example, teachers who want to pursue certifications through such technology companies as Google, Microsoft, or Apple can work through their educator programs. Organizations like Digital Promise (**digitalpromise.org**) and BloomBoard (**bloomboard.com**) also offer micro-credentialing for educators. Some districts are even creating their own credentialing courses where teachers can earn badges using various tech tools or demonstrating certain skill sets. Micro-credentials can be tailored to the specific

Digital
Promise

BloomBoard

needs of your teachers and allow them to choose the courses that are most relevant to them. They can complete the work at their own pace, providing time and opportunity that is unlimited. Is micro-credentialing happening in your district? Share with the #Connect2Lead community, and let us know what is working well.

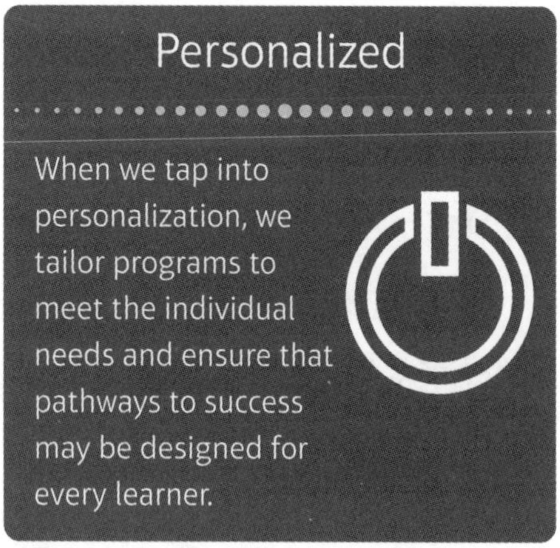

Why Shift Our PD?

Active learning is an essential characteristic of professional learning (Darling-Hammond, 2017). This is not the sit-and-get model. It means collaboration, discussion, practice, and planning with a focus on new learning,

Personalized

When we tap into personalization, we tailor programs to meet the individual needs and ensure that pathways to success may be designed for every learner.

Figure 2.2 Learning networks facilitate personalized learning with each member pursuing topics of interest while also contributing to the professional growth of the group.

such as can happen within professional networks. As Katie Martin explained in "10 Characteristics of Professional Learning that Inspires Learner-Centered Innovation" (2018), many districts are moving away from large group learning sessions and opting for teacher choice in a variety of session offerings that give educators purpose, motivation, and empowerment in their learning. Although this is a step in the right direction, Martin advocated for learning that is designed to support the learning of new information, the time to read, observe, and discuss, as well as the time to reflect and make sense of what has been learned.

The fact is that your teachers can benefit from personalized learning just as much as your students. As leaders, we need to dedicate time for teachers to learn about the topics that will impact their practice the most. In addition, we need to be open to the idea that teachers will learn best in the formats that they prefer (which may not always be the ones that *we* prefer). Shifting our professional learning from the existing model to one that includes collaborative learning networks allows us to benefit from the collective knowledge of others. It helps leaders to have a wider circle of support in their roles and also provides the same for teachers.

Make your new model of professional learning:

Purposeful. Just as students often ask, "When am I ever going to use this?" teachers feel that same struggle. They deserve to know the purpose of the professional learning and even be a part of the planning. When everyone understands school and district goals, they will see the connections between professional learning experiences and the vision of the school district.

Learner-Driven. When individuals are engaged in inquiry and posing questions, they are more invested than when they are being guided by someone else. Within your leadership style, ensure that your relationship with educators promotes their ability to observe and question things, especially professional learning. When our decisions are learner-driven, we value their ability to create solutions and solve problems within the school structure.

Supportive. An environment that fosters new learning is one that should be safe and comfortable. You can create an environment where teachers know that they are encouraged to take risks and try new things. Leaders can ensure that teachers know they have permission to think flexibly and explore new possibilities.

Diverse. Set up the conditions for educators to connect with others and collaborate on new ideas. When we create these opportunities, we expose teachers to diverse ideas and different perspectives. Creating paths for educators to explore new learning fosters their ability to support students as they move forward.

Shifting our professional development to ensure a model that is purposeful, learner-driven, supportive, and diverse may be a tall order depending on your location, your resources, and your school district. If you are looking for a comprehensive way to address all of those components, then Edcamp may be just the model for your educators.

Do You Edcamp?

Known as the *unconference*, Edcamp is a day-long, face-to-face professional learning event that will change the way you think about your own learning (Figure 2.3). Often held on Saturdays, Edcamp begins with participants brainstorming ideas for topics to discuss. You see, there is no agenda, no preconceived list of sessions. Nothing is pre-arranged, which makes for an exciting (and hectic) morning for event facilitators.

Figure 2.3 Post-Its are added to the Session Board at EdcampPGH.

Edcamp is for educators, by educators. It's a gathering of a supportive group of thinkers who choose to learn and grow together on a day that is completely driven by them. It is an experience mapped out by individual purpose through interactions with diverse educators who push your thinking and share best practices. Although this approach might sound empowering and exciting to you, it may make some educators slightly uncomfortable, leaving them not quite sure what to write down and reluctant to be the first one to speak up. There are no wrong answers at Edcamp, as these experiences are personalized to the needs of the attendees. Edcamp is what you make of it!

After attending a successful Edcamp event with a few of my district's teachers and leaders, my colleagues and I felt renewed, energized, and part of a greater movement for improving education. It was such an enlightening day that we started talking about the possibility of hosting our own. We had connected with researchers from Carnegie Mellon University while exploring virtual reality technology. We experienced our first Breakout EDU game. We met educators from all over the region who were focused on innovative practices, established connections with new educator friends, and reinforced existing relationships with others. If this learning was good for a few of us, why not open it up to our entire district or county?

Thinking about all the things we would need to do to host an amazing event, our planning committee began by networking: We reached out to the founders of Edcamp Pittsburgh and asked if we could be the host location for their spring event. We spoke to our district leaders and school board about use of the facilities. We contacted both local and national companies for donations of supplies, food, and funding. Our connections both locally and through social media allowed us to reach out to lots of different partners to design a successful educational event.

HOST YOUR OWN: BEFORE CAMP

When planning your own Edcamp, reach out to the Edcamp Foundation (**edcamp.org**), which can provide a variety of resources to get you started. Reach out to your community connections to see who might support your event. We did and were lucky to secure a monetary donation from a local vendor that covered most of the food for our event, eliminating one of our largest expenses. Our committee also reached out to educational technology companies to see who was willing to send us swag. We received books, bags, stickers, and shirts to use as giveaways.

Edcamp
Host Tips

Create a buzz about the event. For instance, we advertised the event primarily through social media, but also sent out personal invitations to a number of educators within our existing networks. Reach out to local colleges and universities in your area to tap into their pool of pre-service teachers.

HOST YOUR OWN: DURING CAMP

Be prepared to be busy. The morning of our camp, volunteers welcomed more than 100 participants by handing out swag bags and offering them breakfast. While campers ate and mingled, they also jotted down topics of interest for the day. Because our group included pre-service teachers, teachers, principals, and central office administrators, we created a diverse list of ideas. During this time participants also filled in the Session Board, which served as the schedule for the day. Topics for our Edcamp included social-emotional learning, assessment and grading, makerspace learning, and video animation. Throughout the day, participants moved in and out of sessions, finding the content and connections that met their needs.

Don't hesitate to borrow the best ideas from Edcamps you've attended and add them to your event. For our Edcamp, we knew we wanted great food, T-shirts, and lots of fun giveaways. We had a local hotspot deliver lunch, and organized an afternoon ice cream break. Throughout the day, our volunteers also gave away prizes, organized a Twitter challenge, and passed out treats.

HOST YOUR OWN: AFTER CAMP

Once the event is over, there's still work to be done and ways to forge connections. For example, we sent out thank you letters to sponsors and shared posts of appreciation all over social media. We also took time to reach out to the participants—our newly formed learning network. From this one-day event, we leveraged new partnerships with a local university, a tech start-up company, and an event sponsor. The Edcamp experience not only fueled our learning that day, but it also extended learning beyond what we expected.

Edcamp is one way to power up your professional learning, enabling you to build new knowledge while you also build your learning network. It provides a personalized approach for educators: When they've gotten all they need from one session, they can follow what the Edcamp Foundation calls the Rule of Two Feet and freely move to another. The informal Edcamp setup is a bit unconventional (Figure 2.4), but it provides a welcoming atmosphere for newcomers, as well as those who have a few unconferences under their belts. Ultimately, Edcamp is one way to build relationships and widen your network, but it is only one day. A good way to follow up on it is to connect through Twitter and try some of the innovative approaches to professional learning for educators found there.

> ## Unconventional
>
> Unconventional thinking on the part of school leaders may mean expanding your network to include unusual partnerships or unique opportunities that support all learners.

Figure 2.4 Look for unconventional opportunities to build your network and expand learning for those you serve. Connected leaders go to great lengths to leverage new learning opportunities in their schools.

Edcamp Voice: Learning Event and Learning Network

Edcamp Voice is an annual summer event that brings educators together across the world through Voxer. The two-day event offers self-selected learning in much the same way as face-to-face Edcamps, but it instead uses Voxer, a free walkie-talkie app, to enable allows groups of people to connect through text or voice from anywhere.

Sessions are proposed by educators across the globe and scheduled throughout the event. Interested in a topic? Jump in and learn alongside others. Not finding what you were looking for? Jump out and find another topic that will meet your needs.

Edcamp Voice is also a learning network because the groups that are established during these summer days continue on into the school year and even further. For example, the Authors and Aspiring Authors group that began during an Edcamp Voice event has thrived on Voxer for almost two years. Another group on augmented and virtual reality (AR/VR) has lasted even longer. With educators coming and going, the discussions change and new ideas are put forth. These mini-networks promote collaboration and sharing of ideas for teachers and leaders. For more information on Voxer, check out **voxer.com**. If you need a list of Voxer groups, check out Jerry Blumengarten's (Cybrary Man's) site at **cybraryman.com/voxer.html**. For more information on Edcamp Voice or to propose a session for the next round, visit **edcampvoice.com**.

#PatioPD, #FiresidePD, and #CoffeeEdu

It's summer and a group of teachers want to talk about new initiatives and collaborate with colleagues. Let's meet on the patio for snacks and conversation in the sunshine. Sound like something you'd be interested in? What began as a way for one group of colleagues to share, connect, and learn has turned into a hot trend in face-to-face, learner-driven professional development, as a quick search for #PatioPD, #FiresidePD, or #CoffeeEdu on Twitter will attest!

#PatioPD
Resources

Inspired by work from the University School of Milwaukee, Kenny Bosch and Jason Bretzmann created an approach to face-to-face professional development that could keep them close to home and sidestep such barriers to participation as time, space, and personal obligations. They hosted it in their own homes and invited people over using the Twitter hashtag #PatioPD with the goal of learning together. What started out with a few educators has grown each summer to include more and more people, and even headed indoors during the colder months under the hashtag #FiresidePD.

These experiences aren't driven from the top down, but rather are a collaborative approach to meeting learners where they're at and providing engaging personal and professional development tailored to the needs of every participant. One of the best parts of this strategy is that it can be re-created by anyone, anywhere. Educators have adapted their PD locations to restaurants, hotel lobbies, and local pubs across the country. The Bretzmann Group even organizes International #PatioPD Day and offers downloadable resources for organizing your own self-led PD experience (for details see **bretzmanngroup.com/?page_id=864** or scan the QR code).

Preferring their PD in the morning, one group of New Jersey educators decided to meet at a local coffee shop and #CoffeeEdu was born. Similar to #PatioPD, #CoffeeEdu learning events are casual, bringing educators together to discuss the topics that matter to them: flipping the classroom, teacher self-care, great professional books, technology tools, experiences with a new app, makerspaces ideas, new initiatives in participants' schools, and more. Although the events started at coffee shops, they can be at any location that will work for you—food and drink are optional, but often contribute to great gatherings. This kind of PD is known to be "impromptu, unscripted, on the fly" and will likely be a representation of the style of those in attendance.

New Jersey tech integration specialist Kathi Kersznowski has hosted several #CoffeeEdu events and shared some insight into this networking opportunity:

> The important thing to know is that anyone at all can decide to have a #CoffeeEdu. I've hosted many over the years, and each one is a little bit different. A group can be anywhere from two to twenty people who are interested in gathering informally to enjoy coffee and conversation together. Because I plan my #CoffeeEdu events at least a week or two in advance, this involves multiple tweets, Facebook posts, or even Instagram posts to keep "advertising" it. The hope is always to get a diverse group from multiple schools or districts to come together, because the conversations are richer when multiple perspectives are shared. Some people bring laptops because they want to share or learn something digitally, and I've even had people show up with small robots that we play with and brilliant 3-D printed creations to show off! With #CoffeeEdu, you just never know what to expect until you get there! (personal communication, 2019)

Kersznowski credits Google guru Alice Keeler with the idea of #CoffeeEdu. If you are interested in hosting your own PD gathering, scan the QR code for some basics (for more ideas, visit Keeler's site at **coffeeedu.org**).

#CoffeeEdu
Guidelines

1. Choose a time, date, and location.

2. Create your personalized hashtag. (If #BeachPD is an option, that's where I'm headed.)

3. Reach out to your existing network, and share your event.

4. Leverage your social media accounts to promote where and when this learning will take place. Post and tweet to share the information.

5. Print signs to hang at the actual location.

6. Be ready to welcome everyone on the date of the event.

With the unstructured nature of these meet-ups, you may want to come prepared with a cool idea that you can share or a question that you can pose to the participants to get things started. Although you may have an idea of what you want to discuss, be open to a range of topics that others in the group may want to discuss. Educators who have experienced #PatioPD, #FiresidePD, or #CoffeeEdu have shared positive feedback about the knowledge they have gained, but more importantly about the connections that they made with this new network of people. Kersnowski added this advice: "At the end of any #CoffeeEdu, it is fun to just make a list of all the things that everyone talked about during that hour. Whether you do it on your own when you get home, or some people from your group write it all down before everyone leaves, it's always an awesome and impressive list! These lists are an absolute testament and inspiring justification for how wonderful every #CoffeeEdu can be" (personal communication, 2019). Do you have an unconventional professional learning idea? Share your favorite PD using #Connect2Lead.

The Making of a Network

Although many learning networks evolve or organically grow through common interests, sometimes networks can be made. Carefully crafted and developed with intention, the conditions for learning networks can be set up and facilitated for positive change, as my experience with the Beaver County Innovation and Learning Consortium demonstrates.

Building the Consortium

Several years ago, I moved from one school district to another. Although the two were only about fifteen miles apart, the experience in each was quite different. The new district's county didn't have a system of collaboration like I was used to, and I struggled to find connected educators to help me grow. I needed relationships with a face-to-face network of people who could acclimate me to this new area. As I settled in, I established a connection with a county leader who would lead me to other critical thinkers in the county. With each conversation and added connection with these leaders, I realized that I was beginning to establish the network I had been looking for.

Opportunities

Through their ability to connect with others and be active in their own learning, school leaders relentlessly seek out opportunities that will move their school forward.

Figure 2.5 Connected leaders seek opportunities to expand partnerships and create new pathways for their schools.

Through the initial connection, which reached across three local school districts, we decided that we would create a network of our own. We established the Beaver County Innovation and Learning Consortium with a goal to advance innovative practices and a collaborative spirit across our region. We determined that we would start small, inviting in a handful of teachers and leaders from each district. Because this was our first attempt at intentionally building a consortium, we wanted to do it right.

As our consortium embarked on its first year, we identified teacher leaders who would help us advance the mission of our organization and carry the collaborative spirit on which we were founded (Figure 2.5). If the consortium was going to be successful, we needed educators who demonstrated natural leadership, were well respected, and had a positive attitude. Within my own district, I wanted to invite educators who held the skills and dispositions that would help our work to thrive.

As I reflected on who could take on this new leadership role, I connected with teachers at multiple grade levels. I wanted to ensure that all levels were represented but also wanted teachers who weren't "homeroom teachers." I extended the invitation to a high-spirited health and physical education teacher who was a natural leader within her building. She regularly expanded learning beyond her core subject area and incorporated music, technology, and collaboration into her lessons. The opportunity was also extended to a special education teacher who was on the cusp of innovation but was in need of some encouragement. It's important to include all types of educators in the network: novice, veteran, those who are reluctant and in need of the comradery that a network may provide. It's a way to lift up those who are on the fringe but who are ready to be a part of positive change with a little bit of coaching.

In the first cohort, we also included a computer science teacher who was working toward her principal certification. As she was an aspiring leader, it was valuable to have her positive leadership potential. It benefited her as an educator, as well, because she became a part of a grassroots effort to advance creativity and innovation in our region. Also included were grade-level teachers who were go-getters, ready to take the opportunity and run with it.

Profiles for an Effective Network

The members of our Beaver County team came together into a well-rounded learning network. Who should you look for when building an effective network?

You need individuals who have positive attitudes in your corner. I'm not saying to surround yourself with a bunch of "yes" men and women. You will always have your naysayers, particularly around a network that is pushing change, but you will need the word to be spread by team members who will put a positive spin on the work you are doing.

You need hard workers. If you don't have people who will do the work, then it will likely fall on a few individuals who will quickly burn out if they are taking on the burden of doing everything.

You need people who have skills to advance the work of the group. Consider what the nature of your work will be. Will it include scheduling meetings, putting out positive PR, or managing a website? You may want individuals with strong tech skills who can navigate social media and keep the network connected virtually. In the type of consortium we had developed, I also needed people who would be able to leverage our work across the county and bring it back into the district in meaningful ways.

You need people who have power. Not physical power, but those who have the ability to positively influence others and bring them into the fold.

Developing and organizing learning through a networking approach can be powerful for leaders, however this may be a new role for many. Learning to network and networking to learn are different skills that school leaders may need to develop. It means that we are reaching beyond the walls of our schools, our district, and our experiences and connecting with others who may extend our learning in new ways. If your network is open to everyone, the individuals you need most may emerge naturally. It may take time and effort, but you will find challengers, cheerleaders, and champions in every group.

The Consortium at Work

With a focus on innovative instructional practices, our mission for the Beaver County Innovation and Learning Consortium included incorporating Right Now Skills through engineering, design, and making. Each time our network met face-to-face, we were intentional about planning learning opportunities that:

- Could be easily translated into classroom practice

- Were simple enough to implement the next day

- Required minimal materials and resources

The consortium forged new relationships and led to new initiatives at the local, county, and state level. One group began a cross-district discussion of outdoor learning, designing innovative learning spaces with students. Another cohort worked with the Energy and Advanced Manufacturing Partnership (**energyampartnership.com**) to build an understanding of the STEM jobs and the role of manufacturing in the next ten years. A third group connected with Carnegie Mellon University's Entertainment Technology Center (**etc.cmu.edu**) to explore tech-infused higher education opportunities for students. Whether local or global connections, the consortium sparked new ideas for participants, allowing them to consider the possibilities.

Find Your People

If you are in a learning network of some kind, you already know the benefits that this type of connected learning can have for educators. A network can provide you with opportunities to engage in new learning, connect with others, and innovate your practices. Each of these three areas may look different for different educators, however, and finding your place may take more than one try.

A member of the Beaver County Innovation and Learning Consortium, connected educator Kristen Nan knows the importance of finding your place in a network and finding the network to be the place where you fit. As she told me, "I once had a friend share a quote with me that said it all, 'You are going to be too much for some. Those aren't your people.' So where would I find my people, I asked?"

The process of finding your people may include an exploration of existing networks to see where you might fit. It might also include the creation of a new network designed to meet your needs and the needs of those around you. However you go about it, it is critical that you move out of isolation and find the people who will lift you up and help you to develop as a leader and a collaborator.

The POWER of 3, 2, 1

3 Steps to Take

1. Power up your professional learning by trying one new tool that can **personalize** learning for teachers.

2. Try an **unconventional** approach to professional learning and host a district Twitter chat in place of a professional development session. Check out the hashtag #CCSedtechchat or #FSUSDEdChat to learn how other districts are using this tool.

3. Look for an Edcamp near you or create an **opportunity** by hosting one in your district.

2 Educators to Follow on Social Media

If you don't already, following **Sarah Thomas (@sarahdateechur)** is a must. A connected learner and educational leader who understands the value of a collaborative network, she is one of the founders of Edcamp Voice, as well as the lead on another learning community called EduMatch (**edumatch.org**). As a Connected Learner (ISTE, 2018), Sarah has developed the ability to navigate change and promote a mindset of continuous improvement for how technology can improve learning through her school district and also through her connected network as a publisher.

Another connected educator who knows the value of a learning network is **Jaime Donally (@JaimeDonally)**. A huge contributor to the AR/VR Voxer group, as well as the author of the book *Learning Transported: Augmented, Virtual and Mixed Reality for All Classrooms*, she is an advocate for educational technology in schools. Her skills as a Collaborator (ISTE, 2017) are evident as she works to improve her own practice while discovering and sharing resources and ideas with others.

Both these educational rock stars are connected to a variety of projects yet always find the time to support colleagues in their professional learning networks.

1 Learning Network You Should Read More About

A learning network of sorts, the KQED Education (**ww2.kqed.org/education**) website offers a variety of educational media for students and teachers, as well as several ways for educators to engage with content.

KQED Teach

Through the KQED site, you can also apply to join the KQED Academy, which is a professional learning network of educators who share best practices for teaching and learning through different media resources. KQED also offers specialized programs like KQED Quest, an online resource for science educators, and KQED Teach, online professional learning that can build skills and lead to digital media certifications. You can find out more about KQED's programs at **teach.kqed.org**.

Connecting to Standards

ISTE STANDARD FOR EDUCATION LEADERS

5. Connected Learner.

Leaders model and promote continuous professional learning for themselves and others. Education leaders:

5a Set goals to remain current on emerging technologies for learning, innovations in pedagogy and advancements in the learning sciences.

5a Participate regularly in online professional learning networks to collaboratively learn with and mentor other professionals.

5a Use technology to regularly engage in reflective practices that support personal and professional growth.

5a Develop the skills needed to lead and navigate change, advance systems and promote a mindset of continuous improvement for how technology can improve learning.

Educational leaders who facilitate learning communities promote positive communication for educators.

ISTE STANDARD FOR EDUCATORS

4. Collaborator.

Educators dedicate time to collaborate with both colleagues and students to improve practice, discover and share resources and ideas, and solve problems.

Educators improve practices as they connect with colleagues, students, and others in the school community.

3

Learning Networks Promote Equity

I recently saw a quote attributed to Sitaram Yechury that said, "In education, there is a golden triangle of quality, quantity, and equity. You just can't ignore one while strengthening the others." It rang true for me as I thought about the focus we have held in education for so long, a focus that has not centered on equity. With the development of learning networks and the connectedness that we now find in education, equity is a more dominant part of the conversation. How can we ensure that *all* learners (both adult learners and our students), including those who are under-represented or marginalized, have the best possible opportunities every single day?

At a recent gathering of educational leaders from cross-district collaborations, shared professional development projects, and the Digital Promise League of Innovative Schools, Gregg Behr, Executive Director at the Grable Foundation, challenged us with this question and urged us to think about how each of us might extend our spheres of influence to others who were on the edge of learning. On my drive home, I reflected on his compelling call to action. How could the work in my county be expanded to include more schools? How might our initiatives impact more students who didn't have access to technology or resources? In what ways could our efforts to create innovative professional development extend to educators in districts without have access to those opportunities?

This chapter does not have all the answers for achieving equity in education, but it will discuss how learning networks can help and the ways in which positive relationships can leverage learning for all students, teachers, and leaders. Learning networks should be inclusive with the intent to extend beyond the educational learning community to incorporate partnerships and community resources to maximize student impact.

Defining Equity

In education, equity goes beyond race or gender. It stretches beyond language or socioeconomic status. Equity means access for all to the resources and opportunities that will improve education for every child, open learning networks for all teachers, and connecting all leaders to work together to advance education. Foundational tenets of equity include an emphasis on building relationships, developing a welcoming climate, and ensuring equitable opportunities to learn.

In "Equity in Education: Where to Begin?" (2015), Terry Heick stated that in order to have equity in education we need fairness, access, and inclusion in teaching. In turn, that means that we also need learning systems that are responsive, dynamic, and fluid. Think about equity in terms of the three critical shifts outlined in Chapter 1: If we are functioning in isolation as leaders and allowing our teachers to exist in this way, then we are limiting access to resources, materials, and connections that could support the professional growth of our teachers. If our schools lack dynamic systems that provide inclusive learning opportunities for everyone, then we are likely stuck in the cycle of consumption and regurgitation, as opposed to creation. In our efforts to respond to these shifts (and the needs of our teachers and students), we need to provide experiences that lead to innovation and new ideas for all of our teachers, providing equal opportunities for everyone interested in improving the teaching and learning in their classrooms.

If we agree that it is our responsibility to provide strong education for all learners, then equity needs to be at the forefront of our decision-making. As we develop partnerships with organizations and create networks to advance learning, we each need to move forward with equity in mind.

Equity Leads to Quality

More than ten years ago, the Equity and Excellence Report (2008) emphasized the need to eliminate school funding disparities and provide access to high-quality teaching, leading, and learning opportunities, yet we continue to see inequities in our schools and communities. We need to improve access for our students, ensuring that tools, resources, and opportunities are available to all students. Access for all means that we create the potential for unlimited learning in our schools.

We also need to improve access for teachers, building their capacity to teach all children, as well as improving the capacity of schools leaders to support all teachers. Teachers must have the professional development time, collaboration, and educational resources to understand each student's learning needs, and school leaders need to make that possible. Some of these steps can be accomplished through the work of learning networks that advocate for equity and extend learning opportunities that can improve education for a variety of groups.

Not all teachers and students have access to resources, but as leaders we have the ability to direct key educational tools to students with the greatest need. Do so, and do the same for your teachers. Set targets for more equity. Reach out to those in your learning network who are not getting the same access as others, and create opportunities for all teachers to get what they need to support every student. Access to resources means more than simply access to technology *tools*. It also refers to access to *training* to increase teacher skills and competencies in technology and other relevant areas.

For the districts in my region, equity also related to space. Some schools did not have makerspaces or the room to create them. Others weren't aware of the student engagement that is possible when students engage in maker learning. It is not to say that space is necessary to engage in maker learning, but when educational leaders can't envision these opportunities within their schools, this becomes a barrier that needs to be addressed. As we were building makerspaces and other innovative learning environments in our schools, some districts were not part of this shift. All we needed to do was reach out and share our learning, share our resources, and connect with others. Why is that so hard sometimes? It may be because we are still in the accountability versus innovation shift.

If you still believe that accountability and compliance are the most important factors, then you will do what's necessary to move your district forward and leave the others behind. But when you put that mindset aside and realize that we can all be innovative in our own ways, it takes the pressure off. It is important to realize that you need not just your kids but everyone's kids to be creative, competent individuals, not only for your region, but for our global society. Don't we want every kid to be successful? Then we have to stop putting limitations on learning.

When our schools and school systems ensure that equity is at the heart of their work, a lot of positive things begin to happen. Whether intentional or not, links between home and school strengthen. Students will feel more connected to their school and may even connect more with their community, as it brings a sense of collective responsibility to all.

 POWER UP Case Study:
The Remake Learning Network

Serving organizations in Pennsylvania, Ohio, and West Virginia, Remake Learning (**remakelearning.org**) describes itself as "a network that ignites engaging, relevant, and equitable learning practices in support of young people navigating rapid social and technological change" (Remake Learning, n.d.). With members drawn from large cities, rural areas, and small towns, the network devoted a year to holding roundtable sessions to revise its organizational mission and communicate its approach to equity. The network offers support to all types of organizations, but now focuses on those in greatest need. Through roundtable work with diverse stakeholders, and in response to inequities recognized by network members, Remake committed to focusing on Five Pillars of Equity that could permeate through all areas of the network:

- **Learners in poverty**

- **Learners of color**

- **Learners in rural areas**

- **Girls in STEM**

- **Learners with exceptionalities**

Remake
Learning
Events

In an effort to embrace inclusivity, network leadership called upon key members of the organization to focus on a solution. Whether to provide more quality STEM experiences for females across the region with the Girls of Steel robotics program (**remakelearning.org/project/girls-of-steel**) or to establish community-based afterschool programs for teens of color with the Homewood-Brushton YMCA's Y Creator Space (**remakelearning.org/blog/2018/03/01/space-for-equity-in-making**), the network mobilizes resources to meet the needs of the region's young people. Some communities within Remake are more rural and lack the broadband access required of modern technologies, while others lack access to engaging educational programs. With the Five Pillars in mind, the Remake Learning network strives to bring solutions to all, but most specifically to those who need it the most. It has established working groups that engage in ongoing development in these areas, ensuring that their network is inclusive in every way.

At first glance, the Five Pillars seem to focus mostly on student learners, but this idea of equity, diversity, and inclusion reflects the network's intentional work with adult learners as well. The network offers regional meet-ups around Pennsylvania, Ohio, and West Virginia. For example, a "rural-learning" meet-up was recently held to support innovative practices that are happening outside the geographic boundaries of the city. Meet-ups can involve any range of participants, from as few as five to as many as fifty-five. The time is used to share happenings and connect with organizations whose work may relate to the work of your organization.

Remake also facilitates various working groups for educators, school and district leaders, and other providers to work together around such important topics as early childhood education, maker learning, and professional development. These meetings are held throughout the year as a way to advance the collective work of the network. Educators who are part of the Remake Learning network include classroom teachers from inner city schools, museum educators, professors from research universities, start-up companies, and community developers. The network's mission includes the following:

> When learning is equitable, more supports and opportunities are
> afforded to those of greatest need. Based on national and regional

research, this means particular attention is paid to working alongside, as well as uplifting and supporting the voices, strength, and potential of all. (Remake Learning, n.d.)

Remake is a large network with over 350 organizations involved in various aspects of the work. With a reach this far, the organization has the ability to position itself as a leader not only when it comes to innovation and creativity but, more importantly, for equitable practices. The network hosts regular events throughout the region that amplify the voices of all people. They support those who need it and celebrate those who are blazing a trail. In addition to meet-ups and working group meetings, the network promotes events that occur in all member organizations. It is at these events that informal network connections are made, often developing future opportunities for collaboration. Remake Learning also holds an annual Network Assembly that brings members together. In November 2018, the first State of Maker Learning Summit was held to discuss state and national developments in maker learning, and included keynote speakers and ignite talks from leaders in the maker movement. Executive Director of the Remake Learning network Sunanna Chand explained, "Often equity conversations can be simplified to 'we need to help these populations because they don't have as much,' when really our equity mission is to uplift the brilliance and voices of these populations and to get all learners lit up by learning" (2018).

With champions like Chand and others, this network is stepping up to change the inequities in our educational organizations and across this region, ensuring access and support to advance the entire network forward.

Equity in Action

Equity is ongoing. It never stops. It's not an afternoon assembly or a one-time event. It's not something that you "do" one time to check it off your list. It should be a priority for educators, especially those working within collaborative networks. Advancing equity within the scope of your network may look different based on where you are and what goals your network sets.

Within your learning network, make sure that you create opportunities for teachers who are in schools that may not have access to the materials and resources that they need to learn and grow. When you better equip teachers, you take another step closer to ensuring that students have all of the advantages necessary to succeed. We need to make sure that schools are fully connected to broadband, and that students have devices that they can use inside and outside of school so that they have the opportunities to do their homework, do their research, and find ways of solving challenges. It is imperative that all students have access to these kinds of rich learning opportunities. Equity, diversity, and inclusion are critical at all levels. Use the Equity Checklist (Table 3.1) as a gauge to determine where your school system and your network are when it comes to equity.

EQUITY CHECKLIST   Table 3.1

- ◯ Does your school system have an awareness of the importance of equity, diversity, and inclusion?

- ◯ Are you engaged in conversations around equity in school?

- ◯ Has the school/district taken steps to increase equity, diversity, and inclusion for:
  - ◯ Students?
  - ◯ Staff?
  - ◯ Community?

- ◯ Does your network include a variety of individuals that are from different groups, including education, business, and technology?

- ◯ Within your network, do the members represent different races, cultures, ethnicities, and beliefs?

- ◯ Do you build relationships with others outside of your network?

- ◯ Is your learning isolated?

- ◯ Do you share your work with others and has it impacted people beyond yourself?

Inclusive innovation is a choice, an action that we must consciously take to provide all learners with equal access to tools, resources, or services. This happens through the infusion of new ideas, collaborative people, and relevant technology. Inclusive innovation means using our social capital to meet complex challenges. It means inviting people in who may have been on the fringe.

What does it take to accomplish this? Ask Inclusive Innovation Pittsburgh (**weinnovatepgh.net**). Focusing on city-wide equity and engagement, this civic organization described its community-driven initiatives as "plans and programs [that] overlap, intertwine, and build from one another demonstrating the multitude of individuals working for an inclusive, diverse, innovative and resilient future for our city" (n.d.).Think for a minute about the key points within that statement and align it with the work in our schools. When we create an inclusive learning network, the people inside of it are connected. Their ideas may overlap and create an intertwined web of programs, goals, and initiatives.

How Can Learning Networks Address Equity?

Learning networks embody and magnify the idea behind the proverb "it takes a village to raise a child." Learning networks take the stance that everyone deserves to learn the best and most relevant information, be exposed to the same tools, and hear from experts who can push their thinking. In some networks, there may be formal leaders, but everyone comes to the table as learners and contributors (Figure 3.1).

Welcoming

When we are welcoming, we think about those who are on the fringe and design strategies that will intentionally bring them into the learning.

Figure 3.1 With equity in mind, seek to welcome others into your learning network.

Consider the potential ways that we can focus on equity in relation to the POWER UP Framework through our learning networks. With equity in mind, we are welcoming all learners, both in the way we include educators in our networks and the way that teachers welcome every student into their classroom. Attention to equity empowers individuals and groups to build relationships and establish partnerships across organizations that can benefit all learners. Learning networks thrive, in part due to the opportunities for learners to engage in dialogue around important issues.

We all need time and opportunity to learn, improve our practices, and transform our schools. It doesn't matter if you have struggling students or striving students; they all deserve access. So let's break down barriers and provide opportunities for all learners. Through our connections as leaders, for instance, we might create broader access to leveled course work by sharing resources with another district or leveraging technology to access quality open educational resources (OER).

In their book *Building Equity* (2017), Smith, Pumpian, Frey, and Fisher discuss the importance of several components when it comes to addressing equity. They call attention to the physical integration of all to ensure inclusivity to promote a climate that supports social-emotional growth and development (p. 14-16). When individuals' needs are met, they are open to the opportunity to learn and access the curriculum, which can lead to engaged and inspired learners who have a voice in their learning.

When we take the time to build equity, we are inviting others in and building capacity. As we do this within our schools, we may find direct strategies to address equity, but we may also find indirect pathways that can also increase equity, diversity, and inclusion within our educational systems. Some schools are finding that the instructional strategies that provide access to meaningful, hands-on learning opportunities have leveled the playing field and increased inclusive and equitable practices within their schools. Learning networks that embrace creativity and innovation can provide equitable experiences for those involved. For teachers, innovative practices learned through the learning network can create more equitable experiences for students.

In schools where making is embraced, for example, students feel more willing to take risks and investigate new ideas (Bevan & Ryoo, 2016). It creates an inclusive culture that supports innovative learning for all. Making has the ability to pull in learners who don't speak the same language or have the same set of skills. Making is a universal language—everyone can be involved. It promotes inquiry and curiosity for all. The creation of makerspaces and the design of maker learning lends itself to the idea of a learning network. Gathering together in a makerspace presents opportunities to address equity within your school or your learning network.

Making can enhance both a community of learners and the equity within that community. This is evident in the Rochester Area School District (see the "POWER UP Case Study"), where educators have used the power of their learning network to leverage the opportunities for those in their school community. Over the last three years, their ability to connect has increased, causing teachers to reflect on engaging teaching and learning.

POWER UP Case Study:
Rochester Area School District

A one-campus school district, the Rochester Area School District serves 800 students in grades K–12. With a free and reduced lunch rate at over 95%, the district had not experienced some of the opportunities of other districts in its area and was often on the fringe of new initiatives. Rochester's superintendent, Dr. Jane Bovalino, and her team decided to change that and have taken great strides to put their district in the center of some innovative practices. One of the first steps was to join the Beaver County Innovation and Learning Consortium (BCILC, see Chapter 6). As a founding organization within the BCILC, Rochester engaged in developing a makerspace on its campus and infusing maker-centered learning into its classrooms. Under Dr. Bovalino's research, the school leaders and educators began looking for ways to expand the learning that was happening within their learning network and share it with their school community.

With an eye on equity, the team sought out ways to be more inclusive in their making practices and to bring the community into the school. Hosting maker education events like Designing with Dad and Making with Mom, the district advanced the mission around making while also supporting the foundational tenets of equity. Not only do events like these invite others into the learning, but they also open the possibilities for mentorship, collaboration, and community building.

Whether they foster participation in an innovative opportunity or offer access to the latest educational materials, learning networks can help schools position themselves and open doors to opportunities. When the Rochester School

District began its work with a local learning network, its educators didn't have access to a lot of the materials that other districts were using. They also didn't have regular access to collaborative personal learning that would advance their thinking. Their involvement in a learning network connected them to other educators and increased their access to new opportunities.

The new makerspaces gave the district's students access to challenging, interest-based learning. With an approach that emphasized Right Now Skills, maker learning built soft skills for students and allowed them to learn from their strengths. The district's involvement with the BCILC built collective efficacy within educational teams across the Rochester campus, as well as across the community. If there are only a few engaged and inspired learners in your school, there's no equity, but when a campus-wide change is in motion, then you have momentum!

What Does Equity Look Like in the Classroom for Our Students?

Schools and classrooms across the country look and sound different based on where they are located and the people in them. Through the lenses of equity, diversity, and inclusion, classrooms do have things in common. There are certain aspects of the learning environment and the instructional strategies that can promote equity in our classrooms. For example, learning environments that are flexible show that all students are welcome. Equitable classrooms ensure that everyone can access the learning materials with everything arranged in a way that allows for visibility of information. The physical space can send a message that the classrooms foster collaboration and connections among learners.

How Can Instructional Strategies Demonstrate Equity?

When we are intentional about the inclusive strategies that we use in our classroom, we are paying attention to equity. Consider engaging students in conversation in a way that makes learning visible. As you design lessons, provide multiple entry points into the learning so if one pathway doesn't make sense for a student, they can choose another one. Try to infuse open-ended activities that offer students voice and choice in the learning. When they choose, they build ownership over the learning, which empowers learners to test their own ideas and dive into self-selected projects. These steps can open new doors for students.

Drew's Story: An Example of Equity in the Classroom

Drew was a high school student who wasn't exactly on the wrong path—he just wasn't on the right one. This was by no fault of his own; it was the nature of the education system that put him on this path. An average-achieving student, Drew was placed in the lower tracks of all of his academic courses. He did okay, and that was what people expected from him—just okay.

SeaPerch Resources

A new program at his school would take Drew from being just okay to being a rock star! The shift started when two teachers attended a workshop on the SeaPerch program (**seaperch.org**), sponsored by the U.S. Navy. The program offers teams of students the opportunity to design and build underwater, remote-operated vehicles (ROVs) in their classrooms, educational tech shops, and makerspaces. Assembling these vehicles requires knowledge and skills in engineering, soldering, and circuitry. The program culminates in a competition that requires skills in engineering, robotics, communication, problem solving, and creativity. Although Drew didn't always shine in his academic classes, his hands-on skills and mechanical know-how made him an asset for the SeaPerch team. The project started in a general science course, involving students who wouldn't necessarily have participated in this type of competition. They designed and built the base structure. The project evolved as students in a physics class analyzed the design and made adaptations. It progressed further with soldering and circuitry work happening in another class. Advanced science students worked on the programming and troubleshooting stage of the project. The project pulled in students from several different classes and tapped into their skills and interests. For Drew and other students like him, the project represented the chance to be included in work that wouldn't have traditionally been offered to them.

Prior to participating in this program, Drew's school didn't have access to these materials. Through grants and teacher efforts, however, the school began to acquire the necessary materials and created a learning space to support the work of the Sea-Perch team. Once teams had built their models, the next phase of the work included piloting the vehicles amidst a series of underwater obstacles, which took patience and perseverance. Most ROVs weren't successful the first time, and the teams put in a lot of time and energy creating new iterations of their original models.

The competition also includes a communications segment in which teams present their designs, discuss their challenges, and detail their learning process. Although often quiet in large groups, Drew spoke passionately about the work of his team. He answered questions and explained how the team solved problems. Drew became the leader of his group and led his team to local and regional awards. He found his niche in an unconventional program. Had the teachers in his school not carved out this path, he would have remained on the same path on the track to average.

This is only one of many stories of learners finding their way when we focus on equitable learning experiences. When we are connected as leaders, we can create opportunities that are inclusive and represent the diverse needs of those we serve. The power of learning networks can provide us with ideas, resources, and motivation to make equity, diversity, and inclusion a priority within our schools.

The POWER of 3, 2, 1

3 Steps to Take

1. Use the "Equity Checklist" in Table 3.1 as a guide to determine how you might create a more **welcoming** and inclusive environment in your school or district.

2. Evaluate the educational programming in your school district to determine if equitable **opportunities** are available to all teachers and students.

3. Develop a **personalized** plan to increase equity in your building. Tweet out an idea using the hashtag #Connect2Lead.

2 Educators to Follow on Twitter

Michelle King (@LrningInstigatr) is a strong voice for equity within the Remake Learning network. Critical in the development of the Five Pillars, Michelle is a connected educator passionate about advancing education for the betterment of all. As an Equity and Citizenship Advocate (ISTE, 2018), Michelle leads a local working group to focus on diversity, access, and inclusion. She provides profes-sional learning and consultation to educational groups looking to foster empa-thetic organizations and promote social justice in and out of school settings.

As moderator of the recent #HackLearning Twitter chat, Washington, D.C–based educator and author **John Krownapple (@JKrownapple)** shared great resources that focused on equity, diversity, and inclusion in schools. His book, ***Guiding Teams to Excellence With Equity***, focuses on leading with cultural proficiency in mind. John's work as a Citizen (ISTE, 2017) includes his contributions to various learning networks in an effort to inspire all learners to be positive digital citizens.

1 Learning Network to Learn More About

One way that we can ensure more equitable school experiences for students is to provide options for personalized learning. This is a strategy that is gaining traction for school districts hoping to provide rigorous and relevant learning experiences for all students. The **Pittsburgh Personalized Learning Network** includes a num-ber of school districts working to facilitate dialogue about personalized learn-ing. Recognizing the importance of shifting their practices, this group decided to tackle the idea of personalizing professional learning together. Turning your professional development plan around is no small task, but the collaboration across multiple districts provided the collective knowledge and expertise to come up with a solution to this complex problem. The network hosts events and regular "meet-ups" to facilitate dialogue and discuss their programs by sharing successes, issues, and lessons learned.

The Pittsburgh Personalized Learning Network believes that this personalized approach will break down barriers to student learning. With the fast pace of technology and the shifting economy, micro-credentialing can advance student learning. Traditional structures of classrooms, courses, and time schedules are evolving so that students can make choices about what, when, and where they will learn. No longer will students need to be limited by a forty-two-minute period or an eight-unit curriculum. Micro-credentialing will provide unlimited access to information that students (and teachers) can use. The group continues to work collaboratively on ways to increase personalized learning options for students and teachers. You can follow their journey on Twitter at **@PLPGH18**.

Connecting to Standards

ISTE STANDARD FOR EDUCATION LEADERS

1. Equity and Citizenship Advocate.

Leaders use technology to increase equity, inclusion, and digital citizenship practices. Education leaders:

1a Ensure that all students have skilled teachers who actively use technology to meet student learning needs.

1b Ensure all students have access to the technology and connectivity necessary to participate in authentic and engaging learning opportunities.

1c Model digital citizenship by critically evaluating online resources, engaging in civil discourse online and using digital tools to contribute to positive social change.

1d Cultivate responsible online behavior, including the safe, ethical and legal use of technology.

Learning networks promote and sustain a culture that supports rigorous and relevant learning for all.

ISTE STANDARD FOR EDUCATORS

3. Citizen.

Educators inspire students to positively contribute to and responsibly participate in the digital world.

Educators contribute to learning networks and inspire students to be positive citizens.

CHAPTER 4

Igniting Innovative Leadership

Connected, innovative leadership requires an investment. It takes time and energy to develop relationships and encourage participation. Leaders motivate those around them by building confidence and offering recognition. As a former elementary principal, I know the demands on school leaders and appreciate the time and energy that it takes to run a building. I also know the importance of relationships and creating meaningful connections that will advance learning for teachers and for educators. With all that is on your plate as a leader, it is hard for me to ask you to add more to it—but taking time to make connections is just that important. This chapter is here to help you. It explores the ways that the changing educational landscape has transformed the role of school and district leaders and offers ideas you can act on *today*. In addition, you will meet several leaders in the field who are demonstrating the innovative leadership needed to move their school systems forward.

School Leaders Matter

Principals make a difference in what happens in their schools. As school leaders, you have the power to impact teachers who instruct students each and every day. Innovative leaders give permission to try new things, encourage teacher leaders, and provide support to new initiatives. With innovation in mind, principals also need to be ready to join in and learn alongside teachers and students. Your teachers look to you to show them the way, but that doesn't mean you have to be a lone oracle who knows all the answers, all the time. It does mean you need to know when and how to reach out to other leaders who are moving in the same innovative directions in order to expand your understanding.

When I served as an elementary principal, for example, I felt that my school was moving in the right direction. Teachers were willing to take risks and try new technologies. We embraced collaboration and found ways to connect within our school. When I was invited to apply for a grant focused on STEAM learning and maker education, the topic intrigued me, but I really didn't know much about how to incorporate it into my school. How could I build my own knowledge in this emerging topic so that I could lead the teachers in my school? This became a tipping point of sorts for me. I realized to find the answers my teachers would need from me, I needed to connect with other leaders innovating with STEAM and making.

Powerful learning does not happen in isolation—not for our students, not for educators, and not for leaders. Creating meaningful professional learning through educational networks can leverage innovative practices for teachers and leaders. To be connected leaders, we can use several strategies to better prepare ourselves and our teachers to use collaborative tools to advance learning. Being a learner, leading by example, and sharing the importance of learning are all ways that leaders can create a community of learners. Take a closer look.

#Connect2Lead Educator:
Joe Sanfelippo

Central office administrators can have an impact, too. As school and district administrators, it is our responsibility to communicate a vision for collaboration. The vision needs to be shared often and widely, and in a way that demonstrates the importance of being connected educators. For inspiration, check out the work of Joe Sanfelippo (@Joe_Sanfelippo), Superintendent of the Fall Creek School District. Among many other collaborative projects, he co-hosts the *Hacking Leadership* podcast (**hacklead.org/podcast**) and posts weekly, one-minute Leadership Challenge videos on his website at

jsanfelippo.com/leadership-challenge. Joe speaks to educators across the country, spreading the word about the importance of being connected and the lasting impact that can have on teachers and students. His district hashtag, #GoCrickets, is one way for his school community to stay in touch with what's happening in the district. Through his learning network, he models the power of being connected for all of the people in his district in Fall Creek, Wisconsin.

Be a Learner

As leaders, we are so busy ensuring that our students are taken care of and that our teachers are thriving that sometimes we forget to take care of ourselves. We need to be learners, too, and invest in our own development. Taking time to explore new tools, read blogs, and advance your own learning will help you to help others. With the demands of educational leadership, how will you do this? Try to:

- Carve out time each day to devote to reading an educational blog (see Table 4.1).

- Spend one period each week in a tech class learning from the students.

- Follow one new educator on social media each week.

- Tweet out about something new that you are learning and tag your staff.

Lead by Example

When you commit to being a learner, it allows you to lead by example for those around you. When you show your teachers that you are learning to integrate new technologies into your own practices, they will notice. Perhaps they will try something new, too. This may be a risk for you (and for them), but how else will you experience the benefits of being connected if you don't give it a try?

Figure 4.1 Cross-district teams meet for PD.

EIGHT GREAT EDUCATIONAL BLOGS TO FOLLOW		Table 4.1
BLOG	**DESCRIPTION**	**LINK**
Dangerously Irrelevant Scott McLeod	Focused on technology, leadership, and schools for the future.	**dangerouslyirrelevant.org**
The IgnitED Teacher IgnitED	Provides real-world classroom tips, solutions, and resources.	**fuelgreatminds.com/blog**
Free Technology for Teachers Richard Byrne	Shares information about free resources available for classrooms.	**freetech4teachers.com**
Cult of Pedagogy Jennifer Gonzales	Focused on technology, leadership, and schools for the future.	**cultofpedagogy.com**
EdTech 4 Beginners Neil Jarrett	Provides real-world classroom tips, solutions, and resources.	**edtech4beginners.com**
Class Tech Tips Monica Burns	Shares information about free resources available for classrooms.	**classtechtips.com/blog**
A Principal's Reflections Eric Sheninger	Focused on technology, leadership, and schools for the future.	**esheninger.blogspot.com**
Blogging About the Web 2.0 Connected Classroom Steven Anderson	Provides real-world classroom tips, solutions, and resources.	**blog.web20classroom.org**

There's no better way to encourage that risk-taking than leading by example in one of these ways:

- Post a quick video of you describing some of the great learning happening in your school.

- Join a Twitter chat or a Voxer group, and share your experience with others.

- Start your own blog, and post it on the school website.

- Offer a lunch-and-learn session (you bring the pizza), and share something that you are learning with your staff (Figure 4.1).

#Connect2Lead Educator:
Emily Clare

Emily Clare embodies the ISTE Empowering Leader standard (ISTE, 2018), using her learning network to move her school forward in innovative ways. As a building principal, Emily has worked in rural and suburban districts. Her experiences and these connections allow her to capitalize on opportunities for her teachers that will have an impact in the classroom. As Emily explained,

> Networking has been a game changer in my leadership practice. The most recent example involves connecting with another administrator on Twitter about an opportunity to attend a local university's research summit to connect researchers with practitioners. I would have never known about this event without my Twitter network, and having access to this event allowed me to provide my students with curriculum in artificial intelligence. While at the event, I met a representative from Ready AI (**readyai.org**). The next week, I connected with the company on Twitter as a follow-up and to learn more about what it offers to students in grades 7–12. After a brief discussion with the company via a live webinar, we planned a professional development opportunity at my school district for up to twenty teachers from school districts across two counties. This professional development will provide teachers with access to the curriculum in artificial intelligence, a cutting edge and critical topic of study for middle school students in the 21st century. Without my network, my students may have never been introduced to this topic while in junior or senior high school. (personal communication, 2018)

Share the Importance

When I interview new teacher candidates, I often ask them a question about what they are reading. Some will share articles they've likely been given by their professors. Others might mention an educational book they've read for a class. Others might talk about a recent blog. Is there one type of reading that is more relevant or one that is more valued by others? Some on the same interview panel as me might prefer traditional types of reading over blogs, but to me, a candidate who reads blogs regularly, or even writes their own, is someone who understands the power of connecting. As a district leader, I recognize the value that an educator like that brings to the district. Part of my responsibility is to convey that importance to others on the interview committee—and beyond.

Sometimes we block out or devalue things we aren't familiar with. This applies to teachers, parents, leaders, and school board members. If the value that YouTube can bring to classroom instruction isn't understood, it is blocked. We can't afford to limit student learning in this way, nor can we afford to limit our educators' abilities to connect with, and learn from, others.

A tech person that I worked with previously had this same issue. He shuddered at the mention of Facebook. He put up roadblocks at every turn when I talked about the power of Twitter. Why? Because he didn't understand. He just didn't see how connecting to others through Twitter could be relevant to students or teachers. As leaders, when we share the importance of being connected, we provide teachers and those within the school community with a potential path for learning.

#Connect2Lead Educator: Jessica Webster

Jessica Webster epitomizes what it means to a connected educator and Empowering Leader (ISTE, 2018). Fully embracing the power of both physical and digital networks, Jessica takes the lead as a building principal, creating connections for her team, but also empowering them to make connections of their own. As she explained,

> Teaching can often be a solitary experience. There is one teacher in a class-room, often one administrator in a building, and we shut our doors and do

our thing. This can make innovation and risk taking a lonely exercise, and leave us feeling vulnerable and uncertain. I have found that using social media professionally, especially Twitter, has helped me build virtual bridges to others grappling with the same things. It validates my opinions, or pushes me to see things from other perspectives. It helps me depersonalize my own challenges when I know others are facing similar issues. You can see patterns and get energized by new ideas and connections. The world seems a bit smaller and more supportive when you seek out connection. Social media helps me remember that "We don't have to do it alone. We were never meant to" (Brown, 2015).

Ironically, social media has helped me build bridges even in my own community. I see pictures and snippets of what my teachers value, what their interests are. It helps me gain insight into what makes people tick, what motivates them, and what they are curious about. This, in turn, helps me make connections and lead effectively. (personal communication, 2018)

Fostering Schoolwide Innovation

As a connected school leader, you need to be vigilant about supporting creativity and innovation in your schools. Lead by example; share new strategies and support teachers in their efforts to move forward. Connected school leaders are attentive to the needs and interests of their teachers and students, and connect them with others who are working toward those same goals. Being a successful school leader sometimes also means letting your teachers take the lead.

Develop Connected Classrooms

Leadership can come in the form of formal leaders who are leading by title, but there are other informal leaders who lead by heart. Leaders can come from the classroom, pushing positive change and innovative practices from the ground level up. Strong teacher leaders connect their students to the community in meaningful ways. Consider a few examples from my district:

- When one of our elementary schools was hosting an open house for their newly launched makerspace, an eager **third-grade teacher** volunteered her

class to be the "event ambassadors" for the visit (Figure 4.2).
The students were able to
choose which area they wanted
to be in charge of for the event,
and several students offered to
welcome visitors at the door
and walk them through the
makerspace. These student
leaders shared knowledge
and connected with those
who visited. They eloquently
communicated with parents,
educators, and even local
media. More importantly, they
learned that the connections
they make with others can
enhance their own learning.

Figure 4.2 Student ambassadors demonstrate their learning to visitors to the school makerspace.

- I recently walked into an **eighth-grade English teacher's** class where students were spread out across the room. Some collaborated around a Chromebook. Others sat in a flexible seating area, cross-legged with virtual-reality headsets on. When I asked the students what they were doing, they explained that they were building background for a novel they were getting ready to read. The more methodical students were conducting their own research on the topic using online tools. Students who were more visual learners used the VR headsets to explore virtually. What wasn't evident during that brief visit was that these students were reading the same novel as students in a neighboring district. Two classroom teachers connected through our county-wide network and then decided to coordinate their literacy lessons and connect their students in a shared literacy experience. With a goal of collaboration for students, the cross-district lessons not only engaged students, but also took steps to break down social barriers that previously existed across district boundaries.

- One of our **high school teachers** engages her students in relevant technology using robotics, drones, and other remotely-operated vehicles (ROVs) to push complex problem solving in unique ways. The students in her classes are deeply engaged in their work and love sharing their learning with others. At a local conference for educators, the students demonstrated their tech creations and articulated their learning, presenting content knowledge and tech expertise. Realizing the value of connecting with others, the **students**

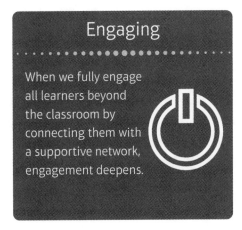

Engaging

When we fully engage all learners beyond the classroom by connecting them with a supportive network, engagement deepens.

Figure 4.3 Engagement through a network means connecting learners, both adults and students.

returned to the district and considered other ways to share their learning (Figure 4.3). They organized visits to our elementary school buildings to demonstrate the technology use to younger students and went on to serve as their tech mentors.

Gaining STEAM Through Connecting

An effective innovator, one middle school principal that I know looks for opportunities to say "yes": Yes, we can try that elective next year. Yes, we can create a club to support that type of learning. Yes, we can start a group to figure out solutions to that.

It was a "yes" that started the work of a STEAM committee at her school. With that permission to innovate in hand, a small network of teachers took the lead in an ongoing dialogue on how to embed more integrated learning experiences into their school of 650 students. Teachers representing all disciplines gathered on Tuesday mornings for a half hour before school to figure out what STEAM would look like in their school. The group consisted of teachers from art, music, ELA, math, science, technology, and special education.

At first, the group focused on resources and opportunities for their individual classrooms. That grew into cross-discipline collaboration and co-taught lessons. The committee, a small community of practice, began sharing new grant opportunities they had heard about and workshops that they attended together. After a year of meeting, they decided that what they were accomplishing with STEAM was changing the landscape of their classrooms. Students were more engaged in learning. They were collaborating and creating, but this was only happening in pockets. How could they expand this work to be a schoolwide initiative?

Their STEAM committee began to build their network. They each reached out to others in their department or grade level and shared the work of the committee. They invited their colleagues into their classrooms to see some of the work they were doing. The group decided to create schoolwide design challenges. Now design challenges happen quarterly across grades 5–8. With a focus on engineering, the committee has created challenges with an environmental twist and others that focus on problem-solving and invention.

Support Flexible Environments

Many classrooms in 2017 still looked pretty similar to those in 1917: Desks in rows, bottoms in seats, teacher at the front of the room writing content on a board, students consuming the information. Does this sound like a great place to learn? Do you want to be part of this learning space? Probably not—and neither do your students. Innovative teachers are leading the way into a new era, and two such are in my own district.

As the assistant superintendent, I remember stopping by one upper elementary teacher's classroom, which was filled with active, talkative students who needed some attention. She wondered out loud about whether she might move some desks out of the classroom to make more room. "Why not?" I said. Slowly, she started to introduce new things into her classroom. First arrived a carpet at the front of the room where students could gather to read or talk. Next came two stability balls for those students who needed to move and bounce, followed by two patio cushions on the floor at a lowered table, then a taller café table with stools. As each addition was shared with students, they became more excited and more desks disappeared. Each change was done with students in mind. Those who wanted to maintain their desk and chair were permitted to. Those who wanted to try something different were given that option. Some students tried something different every day. Others tried a few choices until they found what worked for them and then stuck with it (Figure 4.4).

Figure 4.4 Flexible seating in the classroom provides options for learners.

One day, a student named Dan asked if he could stand instead of sit. The teacher agreed, and Dan found a place toward the back of the room where he could lean against the windowsill. He tapped his feet and shifted positions but pretty much stood there all day. After the third day of Dan standing, the teacher decided to explore other ways to support him in the classroom. On Twitter, she saw some standing desks with a fidget bar for your feet, so she launched a project on **DonorsChoose.org** to fund six of them. Those standing desks became a favorite spot for Dan and some of his buddies.

One of the teachers at our middle school also decided to try some flexible seating last year. She lowered a table, put some cushions on the floor, and brought in an old drafting table for students to stand at and work. She maintained the rest of her desks, but even this amount of change took her students off guard and raised many questions:

- "Where should we sit?"

- "Do I have to stay in the seat I choose today?"

- "What if I choose this and then want to try something different?"

- "If I sit on the cushion, where am I going to put my books?"

Rather than decree new procedures, the teacher engaged her students in discussion, empowering them to be a part of the decision-making in the classroom. They agreed that permission to move seats came with some responsibility. They decided that when they chose a spot at the beginning of the period, they had to stay there until the next period. They also decided that, at the end of each week, they would discuss how the seats were working and figure out what might need to be changed.

Through their involvement in a regional innovative learning network, these teachers connect with other educators who are trying similarly flexible classrooms. They now have a group of colleagues to share ideas with, discuss failures, and celebrate successes. The teachers expressed an appreciation for this newly formed support group (Table 4.2) and are now organizing cross-district visits to check out each other's classrooms.

WHAT DO TEACHERS SAY ABOUT THE POWER OF A LEARNING NETWORK? Table 4.2

My Learning Network:

○ "Reinvigorates my teaching."

○ "Gives me a voice."

○ "Provides personalized support."

○ "Helps me see self as an agent for change."

○ "Offers me a new ability to disrupt the status quo."

○ "Gives me new ideas."

○ "Makes me feel part of a greater community."

○ "Increases my awareness of new resources."

○ "Is an ongoing source of inspiration."

Leaders Leverage Connections

As a principal and leader of learning, everyone is looking to you. The students look to you as a role model and the leader of learning. The teachers look to you for guidance and direction. The community looks to you, as do the parents, learning from your example and working toward your vision. If you emphasize the importance and value of connected learning, you will impact your entire school community. When you say, "I am a connected leader, and I take time to build relationships that will improve the teaching and learning in this school," people will listen.

POWER UP Case Study:
Expanding Innovation Project

A few years ago, I attended a "Wisdom Exchange" of educators at the LUMA Institute (**www.luma-institute.com**), which provides design-thinking training and innovation support for corporations of all kinds, as well as educational systems. The concept behind the Wisdom Exchange gathering was that each educator and their organization would share an idea that might connect to the ideas and initiatives from another organization, and the two could collaborate on a project that would expand innovation across communities and throughout the region. Each Expanding Innovation Project would receive funding, so the educators could put their practices into action.

Luma
Workplace

The day began as the group of educators gathered in the Kiva, a round room with whiteboard walls intended for idea sharing and collaboration. The Exchange facilitator explained what would happen:

- Each innovator (educators, both formal and informal) pitches an idea to the group for two to three minutes.

- The group asks questions or makes comments.

- The facilitator summarizes all ideas.

Then the nervousness ensued. The challenge was to consider all of the pitches and pair up with someone. It felt like a sixth-grade dodgeball game. Everyone looked around the room trying to figure out whom they wanted to work with.

Who wanted to work with them? Whose ideas were compatible? How would the team selection unfold?

Luckily, I connected with an amazing educator in a neighboring school district. We briefly reiterated our common goal to build teacher capacity around innovative practices. We were joined by a colleague from a charter school with a common interest—and embarked on a year of professional learning together.

With training from the LUMA Institute, we spent two days fleshing out our idea. We planned to bring teachers together from our three districts: one suburban, one urban, and one rural. With equity in mind, we planned with consideration for our students and educators who were represented in Remake Learning's Five Pillars of Equity (see Chapter 3).

Over the course of the year, we engaged a diverse group of educators in shared dialogue and professional learning with a focus on empowerment: empowering teachers so they could empower their students. The work initiated connections across school systems and opened lines of communication and sharing that still continue today.

The POWER of 3, 2, 1

3 Steps to Take

1. Communicate your vision for being connected and **engaging** with others throughout your school community.

2. Plan to attend a regional or national conference. This is a great way to meet other educators from your learning network and continue to build the **relationships** that you began virtually.

3. Join in a weekly Twitter chat, and take the **opportunity** to share your experience with your staff. Need an engaging chat? Try #WeTeachuN, #formativechat, #satchat, or #HackLearning.

2 Educators to Follow on Twitter

Aspiring principal and all-around amazing teacher, **Kylee Babish (@MsBabish)** is someone worth connecting with. If something great is going on, Kylee is likely involved in some way. Whether with instructional initiatives in her school district, like organizing a student-led Edcamp, or serving as a Khan Academy ambassador, she is looking for ways to create positive change through her leadership. Although Kylee leads from the classroom, she is an Empowering Leader (ISTE, 2018) modeling technology use for others and demonstrating the power of collaboration.

Looking for an energized principal to follow? Check out California elementary school principal **Jeff Kubiak (@jeffreykubiak)** for an example of a connected, empowering leader. Active on social media, Jeff demonstrates many characteristics of the POWER UP Framework, as he thinks in unconventional ways about how to leverage learning for his students. He believes in the power of being a connected leader and inspires others to look for ways to get engaged. You can read his blog at **principalkubiak.blogspot.com**.

1 Learning Network to learn more about

The **Future Ready Schools Effort (futureready.org)** is an organization focused on preparing schools and leaders to create school systems that support the type of learning students will need when they leave the K–12 environment. The network offers training and resources to equip leaders in their work, preparing their schools for critical shifts in education. It also offers specific opportunities for principals who are ready to commit to becoming future-ready.

Future Ready Resources

For personalized learning to thrive, principals must create a culture of innovation that brings together students, teachers, administrators, parents, and the community to share a vision for an improved learning experience. This will be different from traditional models of education and will require leaders to provide a vision for what future-readiness looks like in their schools.

The Future Ready Schools network for principals provides school leaders with a collection of resources that support the important role they play. Future-ready principal leadership requires strategies to support teachers, parents, and students in rethinking schools for all learners. The organization provides professional learning and coaching to move their schools forward in ways that will embrace innovation, supported by the skillful use of technology.

Future Ready Principals are building-level innovators who understand the importance of creating a strong vision that supports personalized teaching and learning. They model what it means to be connected in and out of school. These principals empower educators to take risks, learn, and fail with support. They build partnerships that support learning in the community for both students and teachers.

Connecting to Standards

ISTE STANDARD FOR EDUCATION LEADERS

3. Empowering Leader

Leaders create a culture where teachers and learners are empowered to use technology in innovative ways to enrich teaching and learning. Education leaders:

3a Empower educators to exercise professional agency, build teacher leadership skills and pursue personalized professional learning.

3b Build the confidence and competency of educators to put the ISTE Standards for Students and Educators into practice.

3c Inspire a culture of innovation and collaboration that allows the time and space to explore and experiment with digital tools.

3d Support educators in using technology to advance learning that meets the diverse learning, cultural, and social emotional needs of individual students.

3e Develop learning assessments that provide a personalized, actionable view of student progress in real time.

Leading change requires innovative leaders who establish a culture of innovation in their schools. Establishing a focus on future-ready schools and forward-thinking educators is fostered through effective leadership.

ISTE STANDARD FOR EDUCATORS

2. Leader

Educators seek out opportunities for leadership to support student empowerment and success and to improve teaching and learning.

Educators look for ways to advance effective teaching and learning through leadership opportunities.

5

Four Pathways to Fostering Connected Learning

As school and district leaders, we need to recognize the ways that we can create an impact. If we want to create connected learning for our teachers and students, we can follow four pathways to make that happen. Each represents an opportunity to create connections, build relationships, and extend learning for teachers and students:

- **Create opportunities.**

- **Fuel curiosity.**

- **Take risks.**

- **Make connections.**

These are not only effective strategies for educational leaders to embrace as goals for change, they are also practical mantras for principals and classroom teachers. The four pathways can even be applicable to parents and community members as they partner with schools in raising our young innovators to change the world.

In places where innovation is embraced, these pathways are evident. The idea behind #Connect2Lead is that we *all* need to rethink our goals for education. We all need to rethink our programs, our opportunities, and our learning spaces so that we can collectively create schools that will support student learning in the unpredictable future. This work can be powered by the ways we use the people in our networks to maximize learning. Let's take a look at each pathway in detail.

Create Opportunities

As school leaders, we have a vision for innovation and learning for our students. We have a goal for professional learning and growth for our teachers. We have a hope for the future of our school community. When we look to nurture all of these areas, we naturally look for opportunities to support them. Sometimes we need to create opportunities that don't yet exist. Part of our role as connected leaders may be to carve out a path for new learning. This may happen in the development of a new program. It may spur from the reading of a great book or blog. It may come from the motivation to write a grant. With an eye on equity and in an effort to move forward, we must always be looking for ways to ensure that our schools have a variety of opportunities for learners to connect, learn, and grow.

Find the Time

School districts plan their professional learning well in advance of when it is actually going to occur. We have a predetermined number of days available, and we fill them with the content that we believe will move our schools forward. We are limited in what we are capable of doing by the number of days in the year, the number of hours in each day, and the space we have available to engage in the learning—or maybe we aren't.

Technology has provided us with new options for meeting the learning needs of our educators. Technology can offer solutions to the problems of time and available space. For example, as mentioned in Chapter 2, using Schoology (**schoology.com**), or a similar learning management tool like Canvas (**canvaslms.com**) or Moodle (**moodle.org**), can allow school and district leaders to offer more personalized learning options, as opposed to one-size-fits-all learning sessions. After signing up for a free account, you can create a course with one of these platforms or use it to facilitate book studies or PLC groups.

Another great way to share instructional strategies or offer suggestions for lessons is Voxer (**voxer.com**), a free walkie-talkie–style app that allows a group of people to collaborate by sending voice messages, text, or images to each other. Another option is What's App (**whatsapp.com**), which is available for Android and iOS. Group members can listen and reply whenever is convenient, rather than having to be online at a specific time or all in the same place. Tools like these can help you find the time within your already-busy schedule. Use technology to stay connected and continue important conversations that will move your school forward.

Give Permission

It is sad to admit, but some schools don't have a path toward innovation at all. If that is the case, where do you start? Don't just start "doing innovation" because others around you are doing it. Find your purpose. Find the purpose of those you serve. If you are a teacher, find out what your students love and create opportunities to incorporate it in your classroom. If you are a principal, find out what your teachers need to pursue the things they are interested in. Create opportunities for them to try new ideas, explore professional learning opportunities, or acquire a new skill.

When educators are used to the routine of traditional education, they may feel unsettled when change starts to creep in—perhaps intrigued but also unsure. Some may stay out on the fringes waiting for their colleagues to implement change, to see what their peers may try. They watch, wondering how the students will respond. They wait for permission to try something new, to veer off the expected path and take the leap.

The same is true for our students, too. If they've been part of a traditional school system, they think they know what school is supposed to be like. They know the routines and procedures. They know to walk in a line, sit at a desk, and take tests on Fridays. When we ask them to try something different, they might not know how to respond.

"I give you permission to try this" is important for educators to hear. But what's more powerful is when school and district leaders give permission to try *and* ask, "How can I help you accomplish this?" Effective leaders recognize the importance of supporting their teachers to take risks. Effective innovators know that taking risks can lead to feeling isolated, so they give permission *and* ask how they can support the venture, such as:

- What resources do you need to make that happen?

- Can I give you some time to collaborate with others?

- In what ways can I support this work?

#Connect2Lead Educator: Tonya O'Brien

Tonya is the kind of educator that craves learning and growth. She needed an opportunity to connect with educators beyond her immediate circle of building colleagues. A chance to join a collaborative group of forward-thinking educators was a game changer for her. She described her transformation from isolated educator to Connected Learner (ISTE, 2018) this way:

> I used to think that teaching was simply just "teaching." I felt that teachers worked in isolation; influenced only by the inner workings of their designated districts. I used to believe that efficacy was driven solely by one's internal desire to be successful. Through my participation in the Beaver County Innovation and Learning Consortium (BCILC), my eyes were opened to a world of collaboration and relationships across content, grade levels, and districts. I relate the experience to traveling from Kansas to Oz. The exposure to various educational settings, the partnerships with fellow educators, and the "push" into professional discomfort have positively impacted me professionally and personally. Because of my affiliation with the BCILC, I believe that I am a better teacher, a better colleague, and a better person. (personal communication, 2018)

Tonya has developed new skills for the classroom and expanded her professional learning community by leaps and bounds. Now working toward her principal's certification, Tonya is hopeful that she will use what she has learned to lead her own school one day.

Fuel Curiosity

When we fuel curiosity, it needs to permeate throughout the school. This is not just for students; it is for teachers, too. How do we infuse the spark of curiosity into different aspects of our educational systems? As a connected leader, do you enact plans that will intentionally fuel curiosity in your school? Fueling curiosity might be evident in the way you plan educational programs and develop curriculum. It might be embedded in your use of technology or the way you design professional learning for teachers. Fueling curiosity means being open to possibilities and staying connected to your network so that you are aware of what tools and resources can move your school forward.

Design Challenges

One way to get individuals thinking creatively is through design challenges. A simple challenge that pushes thinking for learners of all ages is the Paper Tower Challenge. Unlike some, this challenge restricts materials and resources to make learners think strategically and work through multiple iterations, failing fast and forward.

The directions are simple. Use only:

- 3 pieces of copy paper
- 1 pair of scissors
- 12 inches of masking tape
- 1 ruler

to create the tallest free-standing tower.

In the planning phase of this challenge, designers quickly think about what they know about structures. How can we create triangles? Can we fold the paper to accomplish this? Some teams rolled the paper into tubes, trying to strengthen their foundation (Figure 5.1). Some teams cut the paper into strips, realizing that three pieces of paper can only go so far. Once teams have tinkered with their initial plan and made a first attempt, it's time to do a gallery walk. A method for analysis and review, the gallery walk carves

Figure 5.1 The Paper Tower Challenge pushes creative thinking and develops collaboration.

out time for reflections and revision. After a quick view of the progress of other teams, designers return to their project and make adjustments, remembering that the goal is to create the tallest structure.

With time limits in place, this design challenge can be a quick icebreaker or a team-building activity. It can work for adults or students. The idea of a team challenge builds motivation and fuels curiosity as the designers are on a mission to succeed.

Classroom Visits

Another simple way to fuel curiosity among your teachers is to engage in school and classroom visits. If we don't want our teachers functioning in isolation, then we have to give them permission to get out of their classrooms and experience learning in other schools. Curious about implementing flexible seating? Go see it in action! Looking for ideas to spice up your makerspace? Plan a visit to a neighboring district. New ideas will spark from the observation and dialogue that can occur through this simple practice.

Visits can happen within your own school or district, or they can extend beyond your borders. Teachers can benefit from the collective knowledge of others, but if we don't allocate time for them to explore these new ideas, how can we expect them to implement them? Think about how you might set up a schedule to support this learning. How do you embed time into your day to foster teacher collaboration through visitation? Share out your ideas using the hashtag #Connect2Lead.

Classroom visits played an instrumental role in a mini-network I participated in through my local intermediate unit (one of Pennsylvania's regional educational service agencies). Composed of county teachers and leaders, the mini-network focused on learning about STEAM and maker education in K–12 schools. Because this was an emerging topic for many educators, we felt that the best way to build our understanding was by visiting one another's schools. Districts who had developed makerspaces and STEAM programs opened their classrooms and shared their knowledge with others. The practice of visiting occurred once every quarter for two years. What started as an idea shared with a few leaders evolved into a supportive group of teachers and leaders looking to advance STEAM and maker learning in our schools.

The group continued to grow and change, as the needs of the members changed and new curiosities were peaked. We initially looked at space configurations, storage, and content for maker learning, but the group's interests evolved to include tools, digital fabrication, and professional learning. As the curiosities of the network were voiced, we were able to continually rethink and adjust our direction to meet the needs of the individuals in the group.

Do you have a mini-network who is pursuing a new topic of learning? Maybe your group is thinking about augmented reality in a science class, or maybe they are working to transform their library spaces. New networks arise from new curiosities. Share how you are fueling these passions in your school with #Connect2Lead.

Take Risks

A third path to powering up learning is to take risks—just trying something and saying, "I'm not sure how this is going to turn out, but it's worth a try." How often do we do this in our classrooms? How often do our school leaders say this? Although jumping into the unknown can be scary, sometimes taking that leap is a critical point for a school district.

Here's one example that demonstrates the positive impact of taking a risk to power up learning for teachers: A teacher stopped by my office to share a lesson idea that she had for an upcoming unit. She was focused on the ways that communities impact learning. This broad topic was a part of a project-based learning unit she was doing in her social studies class. She asked, "What if we connected with another school district to show both groups of students what relationships between communities can mean for learning? What if I had different speakers come in and talk about the connections in their community?" Her enthusiasm for this idea was clearly evident—then she suddenly stopped her pitch and said, "But what if this doesn't work?"

"If it doesn't work, then we talk about what to do next" was my answer. Effective leaders care about the learning and development of teachers and students more than they worry about the success or failure of a program or initiative. If it doesn't work, then we reflect on what we can do together to make it better.

The teacher's idea was successful in terms of engaging students, but also in connecting them across classrooms in new ways. Her ability to connect as an educator created a powerful experience, not only for her students but also for the other classroom as well. This project demonstrated for students that relationships are important and they can expand our thinking, both in school and out.

Remake Learning Days

What if every school and out-of-school organization opened its doors for one week? How about for two weeks? What if these organizations showcased their more innovative practices and invited educators, families, and community members to visit? Talk about a risk! Opening your doors and saying to others, "Hey, look at what we are learning" puts you in a vulnerable spot, but it is that vulnerability that often enables us to make connections and learn more than we ever anticipated.

Remake Learning Days

Each May, the members of the Remake Learning network take just such a risk and welcome the community into their schools for Remake Learning Days (**remakelearningdays.org**). They create hands-on, engaging educational experiences for students, families, and educators who visit their schools and organizations during this innovative week every spring. Starting as an initiative across Pennsylvania, Ohio, and West Virginia, Remake Learning Days has now expanded to six regions, including Tennessee, Kentucky, and North Carolina. The events call on makers and creators to celebrate learning and showcase their work to the public. Events are categorized into themes and hosted at schools, museums, libraries, afterschool centers, universities, and start-up companies. Themes include maker learning, the arts, outdoor learning, science, technology, and youth voice. Everything is free and open to explore.

This annual celebration demonstrates risk-taking at its finest: Remake Learning Days is an opportunity for all types of learners to showcase their passions and connect with others who are interested in what they have to share. It is like an open house for an entire region that highlights creative and innovative learning in every way imaginable.

Tech Fest

Technology was not a strength in our district; teachers struggled with it, asking for more tools, more training, and more time to figure things out. Our previous professional development plan clearly wasn't working, so our district decided to take a risk and turn professional learning upside down. Tech Fest was born out of that risk.

We chose a day early in the fall so that teachers could learn new things for the new school year. We wanted the day to look different and feel different. We knew that teachers needed ownership over the learning, so we put out a call for teachers who would present the ways they were using technology in their classrooms. We wanted to shine the spotlight on simple tools that could be implemented immediately into any classroom. Thirty teachers volunteered. In an effort to emphasize our principals as instructional leaders, they, too, presented, as well as our central office administrators. Everyone had a part.

We planned a series of sessions for teachers to choose from: twelve choices during each time slot of the day. In between sessions, we built in personal learning time (PLT). During PLT, teachers could spend their time in a number of ways: They might choose to remain in a session and extend their learning further by talking with the presenter or trying out the new tech tool. They might also use their time to collaborate with colleagues and talk about what they'd learned. PLT time could be used for planning lessons that used the new technology. This time could also be used to explore the Innovation Lounge.

We wanted this event to look different, so we created the Innovation Lounge, a space to let teachers know that what they were learning and how they were engaging with one another was going to be different. We brought in couches and other furniture to create flexible seating options. With the help of a local bookstore's sponsorship, we filled tables with educational tech toys (Table 5.1). As teachers gathered, they tinkered with Strawbees building kits and created games with Bloxels EDU. They tried navigating Sphero robots through the hallways and learned to fly drones. We experienced a roller coaster ride using VR headsets and tried some coding with Puzzlets. In other areas, teachers could use 3-D pens and try out video animation tools. In another corner, educators shared the power of Twitter and helped colleagues to set up new accounts so they could tweet about the event. It was a bustling space that allowed educators to gather, talk, and explore in an informal, low-pressure setting.

Teachers also engaged in breakout sessions focused on topics from how to get started using Nearpod to how to earn Google certification. Teachers learned about the fantastic resource, Common Sense Media (**commonsensemedia.org**), a source to vet technology tools, apps, websites, video games, and even movies. They learned about Padlet, Quizlet, and Socrative. They tried out Newsela, Kahoot!, and Flipgrid. The beauty of the day was that teachers were not only choosing their learning, but they were also leading it.

Common
Sense Media

Tech Fest has become an annual event in our district. At the start, this was a huge risk for us. We flipped the traditional model of professional learning and put people out of their comfort zones. During our second year, we had students as

10 GREAT TECH TOOLS TO TRY

Table 5.1

TOOL	DESCRIPTION	LINK
Bloxels EDU (Bloxels)	Video game creation	**edu.bloxelsbuilder.com**
Bolt (Sphero)	App-controlled robot	**sphero.com/education**
Flipgrid	Video discussion platform	**flipgrid.com**
Kahoot!	Game-based learning tool	**kahoot.com**
Nearpod	Interactive lesson design	**nearpod.com**
Newsela	Instructional content platform	**newsela.com**
Padlet	Digital collaboration tool	**padlet.com**
Puzzlets (Digital Dream Labs)	Physical coding game	**digitaldreamlabs.com**
Quizlet	Digital flash card creator	**quizlet.com**
Socrative	Interactive learning game	**socrative.com**

presenters demonstrating the value of student learners as tech leaders within our educational network. This event shifted PD days from isolating to collaborative, and from consumption to creation. Teachers connected with one another and learned about relevant tools that would allow their students to connect as well. Want to learn more or find ideas for organizing your own Tech Fest? Check out #P3TechFest and #P3TechFest19 on Twitter.

Make Connections

Strategic work can't get done without making connections and building relationships. Whether a large company executing multi-million dollar deals or a team of teachers planning a collaborative unit of study, relationships are the core of accomplishing the task. Communication and a collaborative spirit are especially critical to the work happening in learning networks. As leaders, not only do we need to model positive relationships, but we need to constantly cultivate new relationships with others if we are going to be successful in moving our school forward (Figure 5.2).

Four types of relationships are needed within a learning network, and as leaders, we need to attend to all of these connections:

- Teachers-Students

- Teachers-Teachers

- Teachers-Administrators

- Schools-Community

Teachers-Students

Our most important relationship is the one we build with our students. It is the foundation of our daily work. We can't begin to build relationships with

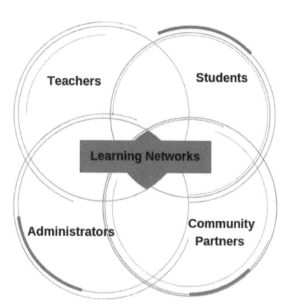

Figure 5.2 Learning networks connect students, teachers, leaders, and communities together.

90

teachers, administrators, or the community without first ensuring that the relationship within our classroom is strong. All of the other relationships will be built to improve teaching and learning for students. How do you ensure that teachers and students are making connections in the classroom? Share out an idea using #Connect2Lead.

Teachers-Teachers

The relationships that we build with our colleagues are critical to our growth and development as connected educators. Supportive relationships among teachers can include the support that you have from those right down the hall, but relationships can also be with those outside your school walls. The teachers within our learning networks can be down the hall, in the district down the road, or hundreds of miles away.

#Connect2Lead Educator: Donna Steff

As a middle school English teacher, Donna Steff has embraced the power of social media and learning networks as a way to connect herself and her students to learning beyond her classroom walls. She has taken risks, supported by her building principals, and fueled her own curiosities in her personal and professional learning. As she explained,

> Probably the biggest and most influential change in my professional development practices has been the use of social media to connect to other educators and authors. Recently, I noticed that book studies were starting to occur on Facebook regarding some of the PD books I was reading, which started connecting me globally to other educators through Facebook. In fact, not only was the new book I couldn't wait to dive in to being studied by a group on Facebook—the author herself was participating!

> Twitter chats are another great resource for making connections to other educators and authors. I have had the opportunity to participate in chats run by my favorite education authors and learn more about topics that interest me by asking them questions and getting immediate feedback. These days many authors are on Twitter and will even answer questions tweeted to

> them by students. What a thrill for my students to be doing an author study and have a direct quote from the author—all because of social media. (personal communication, 2018)

Teachers-Administrators

When teachers and administrators have a positive relationship, there can be a huge impact throughout the school. It goes beyond the day-to-day work of the school. When teachers and administrators have a positive relationship, the culture of the school is one of support, purpose, and pride (Figure 5.2). Cultivating relationships like these will inevitably move your school forward, as everyone is working collectively toward a shared goal. Share your best tip for connecting teachers and administrators using #Connect2Lead. In what unconventional ways do you build that relationship?

School-Community Partnerships

As schools develop their learning networks, they will look to build support beyond the school walls (Figure 5.3). How we establish and maintain relationships with the community can determine the success of our students and our schools. School and community partnerships can support the creation of learning experiences that can foster connections between academic content and real-world learning. These partnerships can enhance school programming, improve parent communication, and offer new opportunities to students. When we connect with organizations in our community, we demonstrate a shared interest in the community. School and community partnerships create more open communication and build trust. Reaching out to build

Partnerships

As stewards of innovation, finding potential partnerships, building and maintaining these relationships, and using them to advance learning are now part of school leadership.

Figure 5.3 Learning networks facilitate personalized learning with each member pursuing topics of interest while also contributing to the professional growth of the group.

relationships with community organizations shows that there is a proactive interest to work together to achieve goals.

School-community partnerships are beneficial because they:

- Enhance learning opportunities for students and teachers

- Support college and career readiness

- Garner community-based support

Establishing partnerships with those outside of your educational organization may be a new role for many school and district leaders who have functioned in isolation for many years. Community organizations, such as businesses or non-profit groups, may want to support your school but don't know how to get started. Pulling these groups into your educational network will take time and energy. The following section offers four steps to get you started establishing a school-business partnership.

STEP 1: DETERMINE YOUR NEEDS

As an educational team, determine the needs you have and the types of partnerships that can support those needs. Are you looking for content area experts, volunteers, internship opportunities, or funding? If so, consider:

Site visits. You might be interested in a site visit for students to tour a local energy plant or to observe a surgery at a local hospital.

Guest speakers. Community and business partnerships can serve our schools through assemblies and class discussions with students. Your partners could be guest speakers, science fair judges, or student mentors.

Career focus. If you are looking for career opportunities for students, you might want a partner who is open to having student interns or job shadowing.

Materials and services. Maybe your school needs some tools for a maker project or poster prints for an upcoming event. Your community partners might be able to help by donating time, services, or materials to your educational initiative.

Funding. Although we probably don't want to come right out and say it, we could all use more funding for the projects in our schools.

STEP 2: CREATE A PITCH

Now that you know what you want, you will need to articulate it in a pitch that is clear and concise. For example:

> To prepare our students for college, careers, and beyond, the ABC School District is looking for support that will help our students become future-ready. We believe that every student needs at least three opportunities to engage with potential employers in ways that will prepare them for life beyond high school. We are currently looking for businesses, organizations, and community groups who are willing to:
>
> - Offer site visits to individual students or groups
>
> - Provide job-shadowing experiences (half day or longer)
>
> - Offer resume review and mock interviews for students

When your team has defined what it needs to support student learning, you can begin to expand your network to involve other partners who can advance the mission of your school or district.

STEP 3: FIND YOUR POTENTIAL PARTNERS

Research all of the businesses and organizations within your school or district's geographic area, and create a list with contact information. These can be small businesses, start-up organizations, or large corporations. Determine who and how your team will reach out to these potential partners. Who will be the point of contact? Will you call, email, or try to connect face-to-face?

STEP 4: MAKE THE CONNECTION

Schedule a phone call or a meeting, and take the proactive step to reach out to your community. Engage them in conversation about the great things happening in the school. Share your pitch and let the organization know how they can support your efforts. If they can't provide what you are looking for, ask them what they would be willing to do. For example, they might not be able to make a monetary donation, but they could donate materials for an upcoming school project. Be flexible and open to the way that the potential partner wants to help. You never know how this initial relationship will grow to support your school in the future.

POWER UP Case Study:
ABC CREATE Network

Chances are, you haven't heard of the ABC CREATE Network, but it is making big changes in the Allegheny-Kiski Valley of Pennsylvania. Including fourteen school districts and such community partners as Arconic, Penn State University, and the Grable Foundation, ABC CREATE is also a regional hub of Carnegie Mellon University's CREATE Lab. CREATE stands for community, robotics, education, and technology empowerment, and both the CREATE Lab and its regional satellite networks aim to engage a generation of learners in technology experiences both in and out of school. Since the inception of the first CREATE Satellite at Marshall University in September of 2011, the CREATE Network has actively engaged 260 teachers and 7,200 PreK–12 students at 90 Schools, as well as 650 pre-service teachers.

With a goal to expand STEAM education by sharing best practices that connect grade levels and content areas, the ABC CREATE hub has focused on the development of teachers through a collaborative, networked approach to professional development. ABC CREATE participant Brett Slezak has seen the results:

> As someone who had felt like I was teaching and learning on an island, finding a network of people both locally and digitally was not just sanity-saving, but also a catalyst for my own professional growth. I am fortunate enough to work in one of the school districts that is part of the ABC CREATE satellite hub, which not only connects me regionally to my peers working in the geographic area, but opens up my world to a larger network of innovators, educators, and researchers through the CREATE Lab's wide satellite network. (personal communication, 2018)

Slezak and other educators have taken what they have learned through their networks and developed strategies to support the learners in their classrooms. They design lessons around relevant technology and incorporate new learning into their classrooms using such tools as Hummingbird robotics kits (**hummingbirdkit.com**) and the Oculus Rift virtual reality headset (**oculus.com**). The network approach has proved to be beneficial to educators who value the connected nature of learning alongside other innovative thinkers. Slezak explained,

> What is amazing, and was unexpected for me, about working in these networks was how quickly and how exponentially it opened doors and presented new opportunities. For example, partnering with the CREATE Lab network as a health and PE teacher, I was able to work on a long-term National Science Foundation grant and present at the NSF in Washington, D.C. That led to being able to work on The Fluency Project, which pushes school systems to look at the impact of technology and big data as a learning device for technology fluency. That ultimately led to me taking on the role as the technology administrator in our school district. There is no doubt in my mind that being part of a professional learning community has been the catalyst for my growth as a professional educator. (personal communication, 2018)

ABC CREATE
Network

CREATE Lab

To learn more about the power of the ABC CREATE Network, go to **abccreate.org**. For information on the Carnegie Mellon University's CREATE Lab and its projects, see **cmucreatelab.org**.

The POWER of 3, 2, 1

3 Steps to Take

1. Do some research. Search online to find out whether there are any existing learning networks in your area. If so, reach out and establish a **relationship**. The connections you make as a school or district leader can revolutionize the education you provide for students.

2. Create one connection with one local business partner using the information from this chapter. Consider how you and your new **partnership** can create opportunities for the teachers and students that you serve.

3. Plan a design challenge for an upcoming professional learning day in your school. Although this may be a risk, this challenge will actively **engage** teachers and give them a strategy to take back and try with their students.

2 Educators to Follow on Twitter

Ani Martinez (**@TheAniMartinez**) is part of a team that organizes and facilitates the people, projects, and organizations in Remake Learning who are grappling with what learning looks like in a time of rapid technological and social change. Through social media, in-person networking, and knowledge sharing, Ani is central in tackling systemic issues with a number of organizations, learning to communicate across boundaries. As a Connected Learner (ISTE, 2018), she promotes continuous professional learning for herself and those in her network.

Risk taker, connected learner, and middle school STEAM lab teacher from Massachusetts, **Tori Cameron** (**@STEAMuptheClsrm**) pushes boundaries in the classroom, as well as through her *STEAM Up the Classroom* podcasts (**teamuptheclassroom.com**). Her interest in STEAM and maker education shows that she is current with the shifts in the educational landscape. As a Designer (ISTE, 2017), Tori creates authentic, learner-driven activities within her classroom. She skillfully uses technology and maker learning to design engaging lessons for students.

1 Learning Network You Should Read More About

Established and nurtured by educational leaders in the region, the **Pittsburgh Maker Educator Learning Community** was designed to connect educators and build understanding around maker learning. Under the guidance of Harvard Graduate School of Education's Project Zero and Agency by Design, this learning network includes eleven diverse organizations throughout the Pittsburgh region. With initial goals to dig into research and utilize Agency by Design's Framework for Maker-Centered Learning (**agencybydesign.org/explore-the-framework**), the members of this network have worked on maker-centered assessment tools. They utilize visible thinking routines and other protocols from Project Zero (**pz.harvard.edu/projects**) to facilitate their work as they explore complex ideas and critical questions around making.

Maker Learning Framework

Project Zero

The network's members use their face-to-face time to share artifacts of learning from their classrooms, analyze student work, and engage in conversations around the outcomes of maker learning. Together, these educators and school leaders are evaluating their practices and building on effective maker strategies that can advance learning in their schools. Check out their work at **youtube.com/watch?v=yOGYqp9JvX8**.

Connecting to Standards

ISTE STANDARD FOR EDUCATION LEADERS

5. Connected Learner.

Leaders model and promote continuous professional learning for themselves and others. Education leaders:

5a Set goals to remain current on emerging technologies for learning, innovations in pedagogy and advancements in the learning sciences.

5b Participate regularly in online professional learning networks to collaboratively learn with and mentor other professionals.

5c Use technology to regularly engage in reflective practices that support personal and professional growth.

5d Develop the skills needed to lead and navigate change, advance systems and promote a mindset of continuous improvement for how technology can improve learning.

Professional learning focused on innovation empowers educators to enhance student learning.

ISTE STANDARD FOR EDUCATORS

5. Designer.

Educators design authentic, learner-driven activities and environments that recognize and accommodate learner variability.

Educators design learning opportunities that are equitable and inclusive.

CHAPTER 6

Infusing Tech to Connect

Whether your learning network is physical or digital, technology can maximize the learning for you, the educators in your network, and your students. Using technology can remove the barriers of time and space and create new relationships. Technology can serve as a platform for sharing new ideas and pushing existing practices forward in innovative ways. Here are just two examples:

- A third-grade class is frantically checking resources, whispering their ideas to peers, and checking a wall map. One team is using iPads to look up information about weather in regions of the United States, and others are taking notes on a piece of chart paper. They are in the midst of a Mystery Skype session: While connected via Skype to another class across the country, these third graders are trying to guess the location of the other class. Their teachers set up this lesson through their relationship as connected educators.

- Seventh-grade students are preparing to meet with their first-grade "tech buddies." They have created an interactive math board for their younger peers using the wires and clips from Makey Makey. Using aluminum foil as a conductor, the teens have created a mix of equations and possible solutions for their peers to answer. When they attach a clip attached to the right answer, first graders will hear applause from the computer. When the answer is incorrect, they will hear a buzz and know they need to try again. This quiz board allows the elementary students to do some math review, while the older students get to practice their technology skills. The students meet once per quarter, sharing their love of technology and building positive relationships across schools.

Although the technology used isn't critical, it provides a pathway for students to engage in learning in a fun and collaborative way.

Educators are using technology as a way to communicate, a way to learn, and a way to connect with others. When we provide students with a learning opportunity using digital tools, we are building the skills they will need to be successful now and in the future.

Learning in digital spaces can be powerful for teachers and leaders, as well as students. Heather Kaiser, a connected educator from North Carolina, explained the benefits,

> Digital spaces promote the kind of knowledge sharing that I need in order to be effective in my role as an academically and intellectually gifted consultant teacher. In these digital spaces, I can connect with educators (in my district and beyond) to both receive and offer affirmation, advice, innovations, and ideas that challenge our thinking regarding educational practices. It has been my experience that the more we interact, the deeper our relationships become, and the more we are able to help each other grow professionally. (personal communication, 2018)

Meeting Your Virtual Network

Once you are active on social media for a while, you start to find "your people"—educators whose work resonates with you. Through their blog posts, tweets, podcasts, or Instagram posts, you will learn from these "Edu-Heroes," and it won't be long until you feel a connection to these new friends. You may connect with these educators in Twitter chats or Facebook groups, and, if you are lucky, you may actually meet them in person.

Last year, for example, I attended a conference where I had the chance to connect face-to-face with amazing educators I knew from Twitter. It was a joy to make a personal connection with such innovative experts and positive educators as Jennifer

Williams (@JenWilliamsEdu), Tisha Richmond (@TishRich), and Sean Farnum (@magicpantsjones). When you have followed someone's work and regularly read their content, you feel as if you already know them. What is even better is when they are just as positive and inspiring in person. Find your people. Follow their work. Connect with them digitally. When you have the opportunity, connect in person. It solidifies your connection and creates a lasting relationship that can benefit you and your school.

Voxer Gives You a Voice

As you probably noticed from reading earlier chapters, I love the Voxer walkie-talkie app that allows connected groups of people to essentially leave voice messages for everyone in the group. I love this tool for collaborative planning and especially for book studies. In fact, I first "pushed the orange button" when I joined a lively group of educators who were reading *Innovator's Mindset* by George Couros. (To record your voice and send your message, or *vox*, you tap or click an orange button.) Each week we posted questions from the chapters and everyone responded throughout the week. It was a great way to connect with my network and engage in meaningful dialogue about a book that focused on the work that we were trying to accomplish as a network.

If you're hesitant to try Voxer because you don't like the sound of your voice, or you prefer to plan what you're going to say rather than "thinking out loud," you're not alone. I had those same fears at first, too. But don't make the mistake of thinking you don't have anything important to say. Sharing your ideas is critical to growing as an educator. So maybe your first, or fifth, or hundredth vox isn't mind-blowing. That's okay; it doesn't have to be. It does, however, represent the opportunity for you to connect with other educators.

If you're interested in Voxer (**voxer.com**) but not sure where to get started, check out The Ed Squad at **theedsquad.org/voxer** for a complete list of educational Voxer groups—from technology to English Language Learners to makerspaces to school leadership and more.

Voxer
Groups

Twitter Is a Game Changer

Twitter is another powerful tool for connecting and breaking boundaries, and it has been a game-changer for my personal and professional growth. As you model connectedness as a school leader and get involved on Twitter, you may notice the lack of titles across the social network. Not that individuals don't include titles (my handle is @DrJacieMaslyk), but the titles don't seem to matter. That is the beauty of this digital network: Jump in a Twitter conversation and you will find pre-service teachers, principals, guidance counselors, and tech directors all connecting and sharing ideas together. It changes the game by creating access to experts and thought leaders across the globe.

The power of technology to connect educators is critical if we are to stay relevant in our roles. As educator and STEM advocate Chris Woods (@DailySTEM) explained,

> I'm a teacher in a small Michigan community miles from everywhere. Twitter provides a great forum to find ideas to use in my classroom. The educators I meet on Twitter encourage, motivate, and challenge me to think differently about how I teach. And I'm also able to share the creative things my students make, do, and say with the rest of the world. I'm so glad some kid was inspired by their teacher to grow up and invent Twitter. (personal communication, 2018)

Connected educators see the value in Twitter and use it as a source of inspiration and professional growth. It is a place to find new ideas and ask questions. Within the Twitter community, you will find those who push you to think more deeply and those who may even push your buttons, but either way it is a tool that you can use to meet your personalized needs as a leader and a learner. A connected third-grade teacher, Kristen Nan has found this to have a tremendous impact not only on her as an individual, but also on her students:

> Through the use of Twitter, I have found my crew. These are critical relationships with the people that make up my PLN. These educators have empowered me to use my voice. They have walked alongside me in my journey. They have picked me up when I have fallen and have celebrated my successes. Even more powerful, they have done this very same thing for my students! Educators from around the globe enter my classroom each

day as a powerful force of opportunity for every child. The touch of a button and my students are connecting with an expert in California. They tweet about a concept, and they have twenty ideas readily available to view from Rhode Island to Arizona. No longer is education defined by the name written by one's homeroom number. Today, in the connected field of education, each child is given a global learning experience unlike any other. (personal communication, 2018)

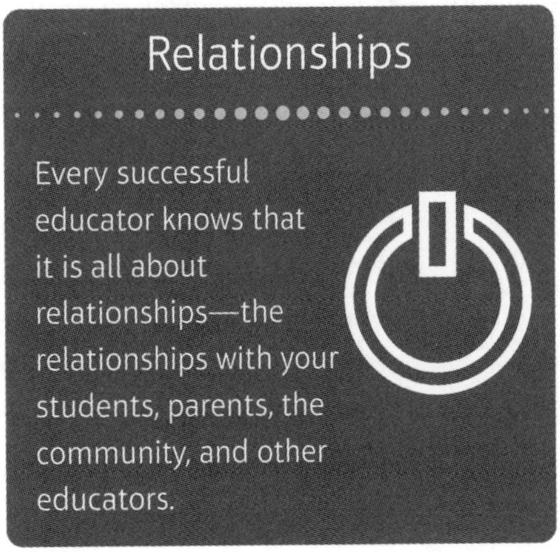

Relationships

Every successful educator knows that it is all about relationships—the relationships with your students, parents, the community, and other educators.

Figure 6.1 Powering up our leadership depends on the relationships we build each day.

Once you are hooked on Twitter, it won't be long before you are jumping into weekly chats. You will "see" those in your learning network each week as you join regular chats and connect with your educational family. You might even decide to start your own Twitter chat. It may sound daunting, but with some planning and preparation, it is actually pretty easy to do (Figure 6.1)

Leading Your Own Twitter Chat

One of the tools that helped me to build a learning network around my work in STEAM and maker education was establishing a Twitter chat. I was an active participant in a few weekly chats already, including #satchat, #TeacherFriends, and #formativechat. Each week, I became more attentive to the way that moderators asked questions, how they responded to participants, and the way they promoted the chat to others. The more I thought about it, the more I realized that leading a Twitter chat was something I could do! You can, too:

1. **Choose a hashtag.** Because the focus for my chat would be STEAM and making, I called it #STEAMMakerChat. (Looking back, I should have chosen something a little shorter and easier for participants to type.)

2. **Choose a date, time, frequency, and length.** I determined that I would just do a monthly chat. The thought of preparing for one weekly was a little daunting.

Because #STEAMMakerChat was my first try at this, I planned for thirty minutes as opposed to an hour. With the busy schedules of educators, the half hour seemed just right.

3. **Promote the idea of chatting about your chosen topics.** For example, you can create images and slides and tweet them out with the chat's hashtag—maybe preview a few questions or issues you plan to discuss. I use the free version of Canva (**canva.com**), which has all the tools I need for creating my chat slides. I also tagged great STEAM and maker educators with the hope that they would join in and support the discussion of the topic they, too, were so passionate about.

4. **Plan your questions.** These needed to focus the conversation and provide insight into the topic. My #STEAMMakerChat is three questions in thirty minutes, which really flies by. For times when it doesn't, I also plan some content to enhance the chat during lulls in the conversation. Once my questions were planned, I used Canva to create slides for each one (Figure 6.2).

5. **Grab your device, and follow the hashtag when chat time arrives.** Be ready for great connections, new ideas, and personalized learning in the palm of your hand.

Figure 6.2 Create slides for each chat question you plan. These engage participants and help to grow your network.

Active in a number of Twitter chats and host of #PD4UandMe, Pam Hubler knows that staying connected through social media benefits her in the role of tech coach. From South Carolina, Pam connects with educators across the world on a daily basis. She said, "It's an amazing way to exchange ideas and get information fast from like-minded, innovative educators across the globe. Twitter has some of the best free professional development there is, and it's often more valuable than what anyone can plan for you." (personal communication, 2019)

Even if you start small, you never know where your chat will end up. The #STEAM-MakerChat chat that I established almost two years ago still continues monthly and serves as a gathering place for this creative network of teachers and leaders committed to STEAM and Maker education. Come and check us out the first Monday of each month at 7:00 p.m. (EST).

POWER UP Case Study:
Beaver County Innovation and Learning Consortium

Now serving hundreds of teachers and thousands of K–12 students, the Beaver County Innovation and Learning Consortium (BCILC) began as a conversation over lunch but has evolved into a five-district network of educators, school leaders, and community organizations. Founded by a group of central office administrators (myself included), the BCILC started with three districts—one suburban, one urban, one rural—and aimed to create a way for teachers in Pennsylvania's Beaver County to connect with one another and improve classroom instruction through creativity and innovative practices.

We mapped out a yearlong plan (see Appendix A) that would engage educators and school leaders in shared learning, professional reading, site visits, and action planning. For our initial consortium members, we selected a diverse mix of forward-thinking individuals: six to eight teachers, one to two building principals, and one to two central office administrators from each district. Our initial goals included three key ideas:

- **Engage to provide shared professional learning for teachers across school districts.** Whether participating in a hands-on design challenge or learning about new technologies, the teachers were able to actively engage in learning and talk about ways that could translate into their classrooms. Professional development that we shared included sessions on coding for Finch Robots with BirdBrain Technologies (**finchrobot.com**), working with e-textiles (presented by a non-profit community partner), and virtual reality using Google Expeditions (**edu.google.com/products/vr-ar**).

- **Connect by visiting schools and organizations that promote creativity and innovation.** Professional learning sessions included an exploration of the connections between STEAM and maker education, developing the habits of mind, and the engineering design process. Teachers from different districts, subject areas, and grade levels collaborated on the meaning of innovation and ways that school cultures can support the kind of learning that extends beyond the curriculum and incorporates innovative instructional strategies. Between our professional learning days and school visits, we stayed con- nected through professional book studies using Voxer.

- **Innovate to create learning spaces within our own schools where stu- dents and teachers can learn in new ways.** An important component of professional growth is learning about new teaching strategies, observing innovative programs, and exploring new learning spaces. The teachers in our consortium visited area makerspaces and planned for the spaces in their own schools, as well as visited the Beaver County Career and Technology Center.

Team Yellow, a BCILC subgroup of four educators from three very different districts, is a good example of our network in action. Over the course of two years, Team Yellow participated in shared professional learning, part of which included classroom visits as the team planned a lesson together. One imple- mented the lesson while the co-creators observed, and then all reflected on it, even brainstorming improvements and texting ideas to each other after hours. These were teachers from completely different subjects and grade levels—ele- mentary, middle school social studies, high school English, and high school biology. They were assigned to a group to participate in this professional learning endeavor through our consortium, but somehow came together to blossom as an innovative thinking powerhouse that drew inspiration from each other and channeled it to their students.

After the initial two-month "lesson-study" project, Team Yellow begged to continue working together because they loved the opportunities to visit each other's classrooms and share insights on how to improve their instruction. They even asked to take on a leadership role within our consortium and mentor new teachers coming into the project. As their colleague and "coach," I was ecstatic about the possibilities for these teachers to be leaders and learners; as one teacher said, "When I'm with this team, I'm my best self!"

Funded and supported by the Grable Foundations, our consortium continues to offer unique opportunities for the educators and leaders in our county, growing and changing with their needs. The BCILC has welcomed three cohorts of learners in the last three years with teams of teachers participating in curriculum work, lesson study, and other collaborative projects, including the exploration of outdoor classrooms, wellness and mindfulness in the classroom, and literacy co-teaching using technology to connect across school districts. We have accomplished a lot, but also look forward to new opportunities in the future.

The POWER of 3, 2, 1

3 Steps to Take

1. Join a Voxer group, or create one of your own. This tool will help you to **personalize** learning for your teachers as well as develop **relationships** with other educators outside of your school.

2. Commit to joining a Twitter chat. Here are a few that you will find **welcoming:** #tlap, #masterychat, #whatisschool, and #STEM4All.

3. Try an **unconventional** approach, and start your own network. Start small. You might just include three or four people. This can be a mini-network within your school or community.

2 Educators to Follow on Twitter

An instructional tech coach and connected educator at the Daniel Island School in South Carolina, **Pam Hubler** (**@specialtechie**) shares tweets about great books that she's reading, as well as tech tips. In addition to writing her blog (**spedtech-geek.com/edtech-blog**), Pam is a regular contributor to lots of weekly Twitter chats, actively pursuing new knowledge with others. As a System Designer (ISTE, 2018), Pam ensures that teachers in her district have the resources needed for the effective use of technology and strategies that will support student learning.

Jonathan Gerlach is a self-proclaimed "STEMthusiast" and advocate for STEM education. Based in Florida, he is part of many science networks and is active on social media. Known as **@STEMigo**, he recently started his own Twitter chat called #STEM4All and blogs at **globaledstem.wordpress.com**. As a Facilitator (ISTE, 2017), Jonathan navigates new technologies and shares his learning with others in his networks.

1 Learning Network to Learn More About

The Compelled Tribe

Developed by some innovative school leaders in 2014, **The Compelled Tribe** (**thecompellededucator.com/p/the-compelled-tribe.html**) started with Jennifer Hogan (@Jennifer_Hogan), Craig Vroom (@Vroom6), and Jon Wennstrom (@jon_wennstrom). All from different states (Alabama, Ohio, and Michigan), these three put out the call for a group of educators committed to writing and looking for some support in their efforts to connect with others through blogging. From that initial call, the network has welcomed more than 60 educators, including teachers, instructional coaches, principals, and superintendents, which are now divided into three "tribes," each led by one of the group founders. Each month, group members commit to writing at least two blog posts, one with a shared topic and one that is a topic of their own choosing. Tribe members also commit to reading each other's blogs, commenting, and sharing them on social media. The group also maintains a Voxer group where they connect on such topics as new ideas for parent-teacher conferences, the importance of mentors, and lessons found in educational failures.

Connecting to Standards

ISTE STANDARD FOR EDUCATION LEADERS

4. Systems Designer

Leaders build teams and systems to implement, sustain and continually improve the use of technology to support learning. Education leaders:

> **4a** Lead teams to collaboratively establish robust infrastructure and systems needed to implement the strategic plan.

> **4b** Ensure that resources for supporting the effective use of technology for learning are sufficient and scalable to meet future demand.

> **4c** Protect privacy and security by ensuring that students and staff observe effective privacy and data management policies.

> **4d** Establish partnerships that support the strategic vision, achieve learning priorities and improve operations.

Continuous improvement through effective professional learning can be enhanced through a learning network.

ISTE STANDARD FOR EDUCATORS

6. Facilitator

Educators facilitate learning with technology to support student achievement of the ISTE Standards for Students.

Learning with technology supports student growth toward the ISTE Standards for Students.

CHAPTER 7

Mapping a Vision
for Success

A network is not a one-time event. It is not a conference, a workshop, or webinar. It is an enduring, connected way to learn through dialogue and collaboration with others. Networks may focus on passion-based learning, new technologies, or leadership. They are a means to seek out and synthesize information together. Our supportive networks help us to identify problems, find solutions, construct new learning, and share globally.

As a leader, you don't have to be the smartest person in the room, but it helps to be the most connected. If you are a connected educator, then you don't have to know about everything, you need to know who to link together to meet a need or accomplish a task. A well-connected learning network can be a powerful resource.

For example, I know a phenomenal English teacher who is always looking to innovate in her classroom. She is always looking for cutting edge ways to engage her students and push deeper thinking. I knew she was working to incorporate AR/VR into her instruction. Although I didn't have the personal knowledge to share with her, I did know how to connect her with like-minded experts in the field. I added her to an incredible Voxer group that I lurk in and made sure she had a copy of Jaime Donally's book *Learning Transported* (ISTE, 2018). Being connected as a leader will allow you to connect others to the information and resources that will move them forward.

Leaders need to have resources, both digital and physical, at their fingertips so they can advance learning for themselves and for those around them. Although the leader isn't necessarily the center of the network, they represent an interconnected liaison to the learning. When you are connected, you can map out a vision of success for your school because you have all the resources you will need within your network.

Start Your Network

If you want to lead innovation in your school, then you have to start by taking a step to become more connected. Find a learning network. Be active on social media. Grow your relationships both physical and virtually. Too often, we get so overwhelmed by all that we need to do within a day that we lose sight of our larger goal to move our schools forward. Maybe you don't feel that you have time for a network, but the connections that you create and the growth that you can experience might just be the thing you need to move forward at the crossroads.

Although an experienced administrator, Mike Lewis, Director of Curriculum at the Beaver County Intermediate Unit, was still relatively new to using social media but decided to give Twitter a try. Now, a year later, his "educational family of followers has grown to include superintendents, curriculum directors, and various administrators." He feels he has grown professionally, and he especially appreciates "knowing that literally just about anyone in the educational field is just a few likes or tweets away" (personal communication, 2018).

Whether your learning network is one that is founded on the face-to-face connections within your school community or relationships that are established somewhere on social media, you will find that networks can provide awareness, access, and inspiration. Let's explore some steps that you can take today to strengthen your connections and build new ones.

Where Do I Begin?

With all that you can do to be a connected, innovative leader, you need to find a starting point. Think back to the POWER UP Framework (Chapter 2), and use it to consider some potential action steps:

- **Personalized:** Explore an online tool that will allow students and teachers to engage in more personalized learning.

- **Opportunities:** Determine one opportunity that will increase equity, diversity, or inclusion within your personal or professional network.

- **Welcoming:** Commit to one action that will welcome others into your learning network.

- **Engaging:** Choose a social media tool and engage with other educators to build your digital presence.

- **Relationships:** Share two goals: one for building a new face-to-face relationship and one for building digital connection.

- **Unconventional:** Think about one unconventional option for an upcoming professional learning day.

- **Partnerships:** Write down one potential partnership that you will explore within your community to expand your school's network.

Once you choose an action step, sketch out what's needed to accomplish it. For instance, maybe one of your action steps will be with regard to professional learning. What can you do to personalize learning and create a connected network of learning for your teachers? Start by identifying their needs. Ask your teachers how they want to learn. Inventory their learning styles and strengths just as with students. Create a questionnaire using Google Forms or **SurveyMonkey.com**. You might even use Kahoot! (**kahoot.com**) for a more informal approach. Use questions like those in Table 7.1 to determine the needs of your educators.

As we work to map a vision for success, leadership at all levels is important. Whether leading from the classroom level or providing encouragement from central office, your leadership is needed to push innovative ideas to the forefront. For example, being connected allows West Virginia District Leader Mandi Figlioli to focus teachers on the district vision and point them to valuable resources in the region. As she explained,

> Being a 21st-century leader means being a 21st-century learner; you must practice what you preach! As an administrator, it is imperative that I stay connected and informed. Not only am I tasked with planning meaningful

PERSONALIZED LEARNING SURVEY	Table 7.1

- ○ What professional learning topics do you want to focus on this year?
- ○ Is there a new skill you'd like to learn?
- ○ Do you prefer face-to-face learning opportunities, or would you prefer online learning?
- ○ Do you work better individually or in groups?
- ○ Who do you need collaboration time with?
- ○ What time of day would collaboration work best?
- ○ Are there other components related to professional learning that should be considered?

professional development for my staff, but I am also solely responsible for my personal learning journey. Being active on social media sites, such as Twitter, and participating in educational networks like Remake Learning, has enabled me to expand my access to resources and multiply my allies in learning. It has empowered me to advocate for maker education and reimagine what school could be. (personal communication, 2019)

Overcome the Challenges

As you create your plan for connected learning, it is important to recognize that challenges exist within learning networks. You may encounter some obstacles in your connected leadership journey. That is okay, as long as you are prepared with a method for overcoming each challenge. Some common obstacles are:

- **Lack of interest.** Naysayers may proclaim they aren't interested and don't see value in connected learning. Prepare your response to the negative energy that you may face. Education is changing, including the way we learn. This shift may be uncomfortable for those around you. Show them the power of connected learning and tout the benefits that you have experienced.

- **Vulnerability.** When you are a part of a learning network, you are part of something bigger than yourself. You aren't necessarily the boss in charge of what happens. You are one member of a group where everyone has something to contribute. This may make you feel vulnerable, stepping back from the role of recognized leader to willing learner. Maintain a positive attitude and prep yourself to be transparent and willing to connect with others.

- **Network Ownership.** Committing your time and energy to a learning network means that you are invested in learning and growing with others. Sometimes those in the network may guide the focus in another direction. At times there may be reservations about ownership and leadership within the group. Remember, there will be times when you are a contributor, and there will be times when you are a consumer. There might also be times when you sit back and just become an observer for a while. There's a time and place for every role within your connected network.

CONNECTED LEARNING ASSESSMENT — Table 7.2

- ○ In what ways is the school already connected?
  - ○ To other organizations?
  - ○ To our community?
  - ○ To other schools?

- ○ What is my role in finding, establishing, and maintaining relationships that will move our school/district forward?

- ○ What connections might leverage new learning for students and educators in our school?

- ○ How can we communicate our connectedness to others, demonstrating the importance of a network of learners?

- ○ What action steps can we take as an organization that will meet the connected goals for the school/district?

POWER UP PLAN TEMPLATE

TABLE 7.3

○ Goal Statement

○ Which components of the framework will be addressed:

- ○ Personalized
- ○ Opportunities
- ○ Welcoming
- ○ Engaging
- ○ Relationships
- ○ Unconventional
- ○ Partnerships

○ What materials, resources, or technology tools are needed to make this effective?

○ What are the potential barriers to this plan?

○ How will you know when the plan has been successful?

Assess Needs

As you embark on this journey to become more connected as a leader and create connections for your school and those who learn there, you may want to stop and reflect on the needs of your school or district. Consider Table 7.2. How would you answer the connected learning assessment questions? Would others on your team answer the same way? What would those with a different perspective or role say in response to these? Consider using the tool at a building or district meeting to gain a full understanding of your organization and how you can move forward together.

POWER UP Plan

Now that you are motivated to connect with others and support your teachers in collaborative, connected leading, you may need to map out your plan to take action. The POWER UP Plan template in Table 7.3 can be used as a personal learning plan for you or for the educators on your team. Start by setting a goal. For example, *we will explore ways to use social media in our professional development plan*. Then use the check boxes to identify which components of the framework you will address. Don't forget to include the materials, resources, or technology tools that are needed to make your implementation effective. Discuss any potential barriers to the success of the plan, and be prepared to overcome those obstacles. Lastly, determine how you will measure if this plan was successful. Use the template or create one of your own; Appendix C contains other templates and resources that might also help.

The POWER of 3, 2, 1

3 Steps to Take

1. Remember that powerful learning starts with you. Make a choice to connect with others and build **relationships** that help your school move forward.

2. Take time and reflect on the **opportunities** around you. It's not necessary to jump at everything that is put in front of you. Although being connected is important, be sure that the connections you make are ones that will lead to professional growth.

3. Use the templates and assessments provided within this chapter to create a **personalized** plan of action for your school. Be sure to share out your progress using #Connect2Lead.

2 Educators to Follow on Twitter

One connected district leader with a strong vision for success and the knowledge to move learning forward is **Dr. Randy Ziegenfuss (@ziegeran)**. Randy writes a blog, hosts the **#FutureLearning** podcast, and co-hosts two additional podcasts—**TLTalkRadio** and **Shift Your Paradigm**—all while being a successful district administrator of Pennsylvania's Salisbury Township School District. You can find his blog and podcasts at **workingattheedge.org**, and be sure to scan the QR code to check out his district's profile of a graduate—a great way to share your vision for student learning! As a Visionary Planner (ISTE, 2018), Randy engages the entire school community in establishing the vision, transforming learning in his school district.

Graduate
Profile

David Lockett (@DavidJLockett) is an educator who identifies learning connections through his role as a Florida middle school STEM teacher. David is a Tynker Blue Ribbon Educator and NASA Solar System Ambassador. As an Analyst, (ISTE, 2017), he understands the importance of data to drive instruction. He also uses data in his work with students as he facilitates learning around coding, astronomy, and STEM.

1 Learning Network to Learn More About

Yours! What learning network supports your journey as a connected school leader? Tweet it out. Write a blog post about it. Post a video on your website. Share the importance of the network that helps you to learn and grow. Don't forget to use the hashtag #Connect2Lead.

Connecting to Standards

ISTE STANDARD FOR EDUCATION LEADERS

2. Visionary Planner

Leaders engage others in establishing a vision, strategic plan and ongoing evaluation cycle for transforming learning with technology. Education leaders:

2a Engage education stakeholders in developing and adopting a shared vision for using technology to improve student success informed by the learning sciences.

2b Build on the shared vision by collaboratively creating a strategic plan that articulates how technology will be used to enhance learning.

2c Evaluate progress on the strategic plan, make course corrections, measure impact and scale effective approaches for using technology to transform learning.

2d Communicate effectively with stakeholders to gather input on the plan, celebrate successes and engage in a continuous improvement cycle.

2e Share lessons learned, best practices, challenges and the impact of learning with technology with other education leaders who want to learn from this work.

2f Developing a shared vision will transform educational organizations.

Developing a shared vision will transform educational organizations.

ISTE STANDARD FOR EDUCATORS

7. Analyst

Educators understand and use data to drive their instruction and support students in achieving their learning goals.

Educators understand and use data to drive goals for learning and for the learning network.

Conclusion

For far too long, educators have engaged in one-size-fits-all professional learning that has limited their potential as innovators. As the educational landscape is shifting, we must look ahead to more collaborative learning opportunities that can not only promote equity among schools and districts, but also equip them with the tools to be future ready.

Our challenge as school and district leaders is to create meaningful opportunities for our teachers and our schools to learn and grow. We are striving toward educational change for our teachers and for the students we all serve (Figure C.1). Shifts in our educational system are creating new opportunities for all learners. This evolution is happening as we design connected learning opportunities through learning networks, advance our instructional practices, and create innovative learning for our students. Find a network, whether physical, digital, or a bit of both, that can support the work that you are interested in, or take the steps to establish your own.

Figure C.1 Get connected, and join the evolution.

If you want to be a connected educator, then go out and make it happen! Join Twitter. Start a blog. Connect on Facebook. Reach out to a colleague in a neighboring district. Attend conferences or Edcamp. Connect with existing networks that can support you, your school, your teachers, and your students. Take a step, and choose one thing that will make the most sense for you.

I hope you will take the ideas presented in this book and create a powerful network for yourself and for the educators that you serve. Move forward and make connections!

Appendix A

Beaver County Innovation and Learning Consortium Initial Grant Proposal

EMPOWERED BY INNOVATION: Infusing STEAM and Maker
Education into Instructional Practices and Professional Learning

Statement of Need

A culture of collaboration is lacking in Beaver County at all levels; among students, teachers, administrators, districts, and community. As education shifts, we want our students to be engaged in creativity, critical thinking, and global connections. Though we are already 16 years into the 21st century, our schools are not preparing students for the future-facing dispositions needed to be successful beyond school. While pockets of innovation exist in the county, there is a strong need to build a network of schools and local organizations that support creativity and future-ready learning for young people.

Project Description

As a collaborative consortium, we hope to accomplish goals within our school districts as well as meeting broader goals for our county. We hope to foster creativity and innovation through the redesigning of learning spaces, revision of curriculum, and the rethinking of professional development within our districts, while also networking with one another to assist in these county-wide transformations. We recognize the need to remake learning in our county and are ready to take the steps to initiate this change in the following ways:

1) **Integrating STEAM Education into the K–12 curriculum and instruction in meaningful, hands-on ways.**
   This integration will require ongoing leadership and support from ILC district leaders, while also fostering the development of teacher leaders. The revision of curriculum and the inclusion of relevant STEAM and maker learning

opportunities will occur through ongoing, cross-district meetings as well as building-level, Google Hangout grade-span meetings. Teacher teams will share best practices for design challenges, computational thinking exercises, and developing a maker culture in the classroom. These learning opportunities will be embedded into the existing curriculum as a way to fuel creativity and innovation. While these innovative practices may be happening within individual districts, the goal of the ILC will be to share those practices across districts and through the partnership with our intermediate unit.

2) **Establishing makerspaces in school buildings within each partner district, as well as the Beaver Valley Intermediate Unit (BVIU).**

Each ILC partner will designate one school within their district to establish a makerspace to support STEAM and maker learning. These spaces will be designed by the individual districts with collaboration and support from the ILC leadership team. Each school learning space will be an inviting, colorful environment where students can engage in hands-on learning. The materials and tools purchased will be determined by each building in order to meet the needs and interests of their students. Each space will be named and unveiled at ILC events in the spring of 2017. The BVIU will also create a designated learning space within their facility. With an existing room available, materials will be purchased to create a new and exciting space at the Intermediate Unit, which will also host an Open House event in the spring. This new space will serve as a learning center for teachers throughout Beaver County who want to build their STEAM/maker skills. Robotics materials, programming kits, and other relevant tools will be housed in the space for formal workshops and informal tinkering. The BVIU has already agreed to devote $60,000 from their operating budget to support this initiative within their facility. ILC partner school districts will be able to host events in the BVIU learning space and showcase the work of their students and teachers throughout the school year.

3) **Providing opportunities for teachers to improve their practices in critical thinking, problem solving, creativity, and collaboration through ongoing professional development.**

The ILC will organize professional development throughout the course of the year to meet the needs of the K–12 educators. Teachers will be encouraged to attend Remake Learning events, local Edcamps, and Project Zero workshops.

Teacher teams will also meet regularly with their professional learning community (PLC) to engage in discourse, participate in book studies and other relevant activities. These learning opportunities will be hosted in the ILC districts' makerspaces, the BVIU learning space, and other local venues. As a long-term goal, the consortium hopes to invite two additional school districts to formally join the network in 2017–2018, with a goal to expand the group each subsequent year. The original districts will serve as mentors to additional districts in an effort to sustain this momentum over time.

4) **Creating meet-up events where education, business, and community stakeholders can connect in meaningful ways around pioneering partnerships.**
We believe that learning should be meaningful for students, connecting to college, career, and beyond. We will create meet-up events for educators to network with those in higher education, local businesses, and industry. The potential for collaboration and future partnerships will be unlimited. The meet-ups may be formal with keynote speakers or informal gatherings to share ideas. We plan to pursue this strategy by connecting with the Franklin Center of Beaver County. While the organization's primary roles include outreach and referrals, they are active in the STEAM/maker community and are willing to work with our districts to bring innovative programs to the young people in the county. Their existing work with developing entrepreneurship will help ILC school districts to enhance their district offerings to high school students.

Description of Innovation and Learning Consortium Partners

ACTIVE LEARNING AND NETWORK DEVELOPMENT

Districts within the ILC are moving forward to build knowledge and expand our network. We are actively looking for opportunities to connect with other innovators and collaborate on projects. Through local events and social media, we are reaching out to forward-thinking organizations and districts.

Individual districts are pursuing professional development to meet their needs in the areas of innovation, technology, gaming, and design thinking (to name a few). Teachers and administrators have attended Remake Learning meet-ups and other local STEAM events. Recently, teachers attended summer learning opportunities in the South Fayette and Montour School Districts. Teams of teachers and administrators participated in the Elizabeth Forward Fab Lab Academy and the Studio A Project-Based Learning Institute at Avonworth. (While we would love to take advantage of other opportunities to advance our districts, some programs, like the STEM Excellence Pathways Initiative through the Carnegie Science Center, exclude Beaver County applicants.)

All ILC districts have a relationship with the Beaver County Energy and Advanced Manufacturing Partnership (E&AMP). This organization provides school/community partnerships and career exploration through business and industry involvement. The ILC would love to expand this relationship and engage with E&AMP to develop new opportunities for students.

The Hopewell Area School District has made tremendous strides in the last year. They are a current partner in the Project Zero group with the Quaker Valley School District. Twenty teachers attended sessions in January on "Developing a Culture of Thinking" with Ron Ritchhart, and two have been formally trained at Harvard through Project Zero's summer institute. A dozen teachers and administrators recently attended sessions on making thinking visible and hope to expand this knowledge throughout the ILC. In addition, Hopewell is working with Zulama and will be the first district in Beaver County to implement this formal gaming program in grades 7–12. Hopewell has also partnered with ISA Learning, a Pittsburgh start-up, to pilot their new STEAM curriculum. A team of teachers collaborated with ISA to develop meaningful hands-on learning with kindergarten students with the potential to expand programming in future years with additional grade levels.

Throughout the 2015–2016 school year, teacher teams from Hopewell have visited innovative districts in Allegheny County including Elizabeth Forward, Avonworth, and West Allegheny, as well as community innovators like Construction Junction, The Center for Creative Reuse, and Inventionland. Most recently, Hopewell applied and was accepted to participate in the Expanding Innovation Project facilitated by the LUMA Institute. Hopewell will partner with Quaker Valley and Propel Schools to design collaborative professional development opportunities in an effort to build leadership capacity within our teachers. Hopewell is also working with Montour and several other school districts on the Global Moonshot project, as junior high students collaborate to design a time capsule that will go to the moon.

The Beaver Area School District has a strength in technology and is looking to expand their STEAM programming. One of their elementary schools boasts an Innovation Lab with a focus on iPad technologies, including Osmos and digital animation tools. They have created a unique, student-centered approach to technology at the high school, as their students serve as the actual tech department through their Student Technology Assistance Program (STAP). The district is partnering with their PTA to implement STEAM learning events for families and the community.

With Rochester being the smallest of our partner districts, the district has faced staffing and financial constraints, which have been somewhat of a barrier to innovation. With the support of the Grable Foundation and the collaborative network of the ILC, Rochester will begin to initiate STEAM learning into their district and develop new opportunities for staff and students.

Through the Beaver Valley Intermediate Unit, area school districts have participated in a variety of STEAM-related and technology-centered professional development, including sessions on Google Classroom, Design iTunes courses, and Engineering by Design. All ILC partner districts attended a recent workshop at the BVIU on Puzzlets, an interactive gaming system that provides a foundation for block-base coding and programming. The ILC will work with Digital Dream Labs to use this approach in primary grade classrooms. The BVIU also provided training in May through Code.org with a focus on teachers in grades K–8. The BVIU would like to facilitate more STEAM related programming, but is limited in what they can offer with limited resources.

While each organization is currently pursuing opportunities in innovation, no centralized network of support exists in Beaver County. By establishing the ILC, districts will begin to build a network of forward-thinking educators who can reach out to one another to share ideas and resources. By including the BVIU, all districts in the county will have access to the new learning space, which will serve as a hub for innovation in our area. It is the goal of the ILC to serve as mentors in subsequent years, sharing our knowledge and best practices with additional districts in the area, so that innovation can expand across the county.

EXISTING FUNDING

Participating ILC districts have already received grants from the Beaver County Educational Trust, Lowe's, and Highmark totaling over $70,000 during the 2015–2016 school year to support creativity and innovation through STEAM learning. Beaver Area was awarded grants to pursue robotics and programming at the elementary level and develop a maker lab at the high school. Hopewell is using grant funding to support a school garden and outdoor classroom at the junior high school and the implementation of "Lego Learning" in learning support math classes at the high school. Beaver and Hopewell were also awarded AIU STEAM grants this year, for an additional $40,000. Both are using the funds to support maker labs at the secondary level. Hopewell also received the Pennsylvania Library Services and Technology Act (LSTA) grant in the amount of $29,000 to establish a video production studio within the junior high school library. Organizations within the ILC will continue to pursue funding and explore potential partnerships in an effort to sustain this initiative over time.

Project Outcomes

It is the intent of the ILC to increase collaboration throughout Beaver County with the establishment of this network. We will collect qualitative baseline data within the ILC districts at all levels by surveying students, teachers, parents, and community. We will use this data to identify additional areas of need that may be addressed through the creation of this consortium. We will collect anecdotal data throughout the course of the year as a means to keep a pulse on the project goals. Through the work of the ILC, we hope to increase the collaboration among districts, which is currently very limited. We will hold a minimum of 10 events (STEAM Walk events, professional learning sessions, and innovation "meet-ups") to increase communication, connections, and collaborations. The ILC Leadership Team will schedule a mid-project meeting to specifically reflect and discuss progress, goals, and accomplishments.

EMPOWERED BY INNOVATION: Potential Timeline of Year 1 Activities

MONTH	ACTIVITY	ATTENDEES
December 2016	• Bi-weekly Leadership Meetings • Create professional development schedule of activities • plan district kick-off events	Superintendents/Assistant Superintendents and BVIU
	• Planning team for district STEAM Walk events • prepare grant submissions for Beaver County Educational Trust	Superintendents/Assistant Superintendents and BVIU
	• Begin online book study for professional learning	ILC district administrators, teachers, and paraprofessionals
	• Attend Remake Learning Assembly	ILC district administrators, teachers, and paraprofessionals

January 2017	• Design and planning meeting
	   • order materials
	   • plan for learning spaces
		Superintendents/Assistant Superintendents and BVIU, STEAM teachers/leaders

	• PR planning for county STEAM Walk events (as per the Beaver County Educational Trust, these events must be held by the end of February)
	   • advertise events (websites, social media, etc.)
	   • invite media, Remake Learning partners, other Beaver County school districts to attend
		Superintendents/Assistant Superintendents and BVIU

	• Visits to innovative Allegheny County districts and Remake Learning organizations	Teams of ILC teachers and administrators
	• Grade-span Google Hangouts	Cross-district grade level teams
	• Professional learning session: Intro to STEAM and Making	ILC district administrators, teachers, and paraprofessionals

EMPOWERED BY INNOVATION: Potential Timeline of Year 1 Activities

February 2017	• Bi-weekly Leadership Meetings 　• updates on learning spaces 　• plan for meet-ups and professional learning sessions	Superintendents/Assistant Superintendents and BVIU
	• Hold STEAM Walk events in ILC districts	Open to the public
	• Pre-program data collection for students and teachers	ILC districts
	• Visits to innovative Allegheny County districts and Remake Learning organizations	Teams of teachers and administrators
March 2017	• BVIU Makerspace Grand Opening	Beaver County educators, businesses, community, Remake Learning Network, etc.
	• Leadership Team Meeting 　• brainstorm potential summer learning opportunities for ILC students	Superintendents/Assistant Superintendents and BVIU
	• Professional learning session #2: Building a Culture of Innovation	ILC district administrators, teachers, and paraprofessionals
	• Conduct Innovation meet-up #1 for educators and community at ILC makerspace	ILC district administrators, teachers, and paraprofessionals
April 2017	• Leadership Team Meeting • Program review	Superintendents/Assistant Superintendents and BVIU
	• Grade-span Google Hangouts	Cross-district grade level teams

EMPOWERED BY INNOVATION: Potential Timeline of Year 1 Activities

May 2017	• Conduct Innovation meet-up #2 for educators and community at Franklin Center	ILC district administrators, teachers, paraprofessionals, and community members
	• School visits to ILC districts	ILC district administrators, teachers, and paraprofessionals
	• Attend Project Zero Conference (Pittsburgh)	ILC district administrators and teachers
	• Attend Remake Learning Rally	ILC district administrators, teachers, and paraprofessionals
June 2017	• Complete online book study for professional learning with face-to-face meet up at BVIU learning space	ILC district administrators, teachers, and paraprofessionals
	• Leadership Team Meeting • explore funding sources to maintain/expand ILC network	Superintendents/Assistant Superintendents and BVIU
	• Attend summer professional learning in Remake Learning districts (South Fayette, Avonworth, Elizabeth Forward, etc.)	ILC district administrators, teachers, and paraprofessionals

July 2017	• Leadership Team Meeting
	  • plan for professional learning opportunities for the 2017–2018 school year
	  • draft article for publication highlighting ILC schools
		Superintendents/Assistant Superintendents and BVIU

August 2017	• Professional learning session #3: Making Thinking Visible	ILC district administrators, teachers, and paraprofessionals
	• Leadership Team Meeting • finalize continued funding proposal	Superintendents/Assistant Superintendents and BVIU

EMPOWERED BY INNOVATION: Potential Timeline of Year 1 Activities

September 2017	• Conduct Innovation meet-up #3 for educators	ILC district administrators, teachers, and paraprofessionals
	• Attend AIU STEAM Annual Showcase	ILC district teachers
October 2017	• School visits to ILC districts	ILC district administrators, teachers, and paraprofessionals
November 2017	• Post-program data collection for students and teachers	ILC districts

EMPOWERED BY INNOVATION: Preliminary Budget		
BUDGET ITEMS	**GRANT FUNDING REQUESTED**	**MATCHING FUNDS**
Materials and supplies for school level makerspaces (items may include but are not limited to: Makey Makey, Sphero, Little Bits, Puzzlets, Dot and Dash, Legos, Arduino boards, Raspberry Pi, hand tools, storage/organizational pieces, craft items, batteries, circuitry, flexible furniture, etc.)	$10,000 for each of 3 partner districts **Total $30,000**	
Additional guaranteed funding: ILC districts will also secure annual STEM Walk funding from the Beaver County Educational Trust (BCET) for $1,000 per district		Materials and supplies **(+$3,000)**
Makerspace at the Beaver County Intermediate Unit (items will include flexible furniture, paint, shelving/organizational items, storage bins, 3-D printer, hand tools and electronics, hands-on materials, etc.)	Materials and supplies **$8,500**	Furniture, supplies, and technology **(+60,000)**
Professional Development for partner districts	Workshop costs, training materials, substitute costs for curriculum writing, release time, etc. **$9,000**	
Administrative stipend for ILC Coordinator to organize all activities within the Innovation and Learning Consortium, plan events, public relations, oversee purchases and district budgeting, complete all necessary grant and financial reporting, etc.	**$2,500**	
Total	**$50,000**	

Appendix B

Beaver County Innovation & Learning Consortium

Beaver High School Library

February 27, 2018

8:30-9:00	**Background and Goals of BCILC**
	• Sharing outcomes w/Cohort 1 Team Members
9:00-9:20	**Introduction of Teams**
	• Get to Know Your Team Members (icebreaker activity)
9:20-9:50	**Defining Innovation**
	• Project Zero Thinking Routine
	• Color, Symbol, Image
9:50-10:10	**Why Creativity and Innovation**
	• What does this look like in our county?
	(videos and pictures)
10:10-10:40	**Team Building Activity**
	• Maker Challenge (small group)
10:40-11:10	**4 Cs of 21st Century Learners**
	• Tony Wagner TED Talk
	• Small group discussion

11:10-11:30	**Break and Visit to High School Makerspace**
11:30-11:50	**Introduction to Professional Book Study**
	• Innovator's Mindset
	• Voxer book discussion
11:50-1:00	**Lunch and Travel to Career and Technical Center (CTC)**
1:00-2:15	**Tour 14 CTC Programs**
	• Carpentry, Digital Marketing, Electrical
2:15-2:30	**Reflect on Connections**
2:30-2:45	**Call to Action**
	• George Couros video
	• Focus on Why

Appendix C

Network Meeting Resources

GET TO KNOW YOUR TEAM MEMBERS		
PERSON'S NAME	**DISTRICT**	**TALK WITH SOMEONE WHO. . .**
		worked in more than one district
		can tell you about a time they collaborated to solve a problem
		worked in a field other than education
		<u>does not</u> teach math or science
		<u>does</u> teach math or science
		has participated in a maker challenge
		went to college in a state or region other than yours
		has more than one teaching certificate
		has taught in a state other than yours
		has visited another school to talk about STEAM
		can share what characteristics business and industry look for in their employees
		has taught students remotely (via computer or robot)

GET TO KNOW YOUR TEAM MEMBERS		
PERSON'S NAME	**DISTRICT**	**TALK WITH SOMEONE WHO. . .**
		has worked or lived in a country other than yours
		values creativity in students
		has visited business or industry to learn what they look for in employees
		values perseverance
		prefers to work alone
		prefers to work as a team
		prefers to research/read to learn
		prefers to experiment/explore to learn

MAKER CHALLENGE PLANNING SHEET

YOUR PLAN/BLUEPRINT

PAUSE AND ANALYZE

What's working and what isn't?	What will we do differently?

Reflect: Did your implemented changes help? What would have been more beneficial? If you had more time or different materials, what would you do?

References

Catapano, J. (n.d.). Technology in the classroom: The connected teacher. *Shift Hub*. Retrieved from **www.teachhub.com/ technology-classroom-connected-teacher**

Chand, S. (2018, November). Speech presented at the State of Maker Learning Summit, Pittsburgh, PA.

Donally, J. (2018). *Learning transported: Augmented, virtual and mixed reality for all classrooms*. Portland, OR: International Society for Technology in Education.

Gloor, P. (2017). *Swarm leadership and the collective mind: Using collaborative innovation networks to build a better business.* London, UK: Emerald Publishing.

Gutierrez, K. (2016, June 21). What are personal learning networks? [Blog post]. Retrieved from **www.shiftelearning.com/blog/personal-learning-networks**

Heick, T. (2015). Equity in education: Where to begin [Blog post]. Retrieved from **www.edutopia.org/blog/equity-education-where-to-begin-terry-heick**

International Society for Technology in Education. (2018). *ISTE Standards for Education Leaders*. Retrieved from **www.iste.org/standards/ for-education-leaders**

International Society for Technology in Education. (2017). *ISTE Standards for Educators*. Retrieved from **www.iste.org/standards/for-educators**

International Society for Technology in Education. (2016). *ISTE Standards for Students*. Retrieved from **www.iste.org/standards/for-students**

Martin, K. (2018, January 28). 10 characteristics of professional learning that inspires learner-centered innovation [Blog post]. Retrieved from **katielmartin.com/2018/01/28/10-characteristics-of-professional-learning-that-inspires-learner-centered-innovation**

Mattson, K. (2017). *Digital citizenship in action*. Portland, OR: International Society for Technology in Education.

Smith, D., Frey, N., Pumpian, I., & Fisher, D. (2017). *Building equity: Policies and practices to empower all learners.* Alexandria, VA: Association for Supervision and Curriculum Development.

Wagner, M. (2012). Personal learning networks for educators: 10 Tips [Blog post]. Retrieved from **www.gettingsmart.com/2012/01/ personal-learning-networks-for-educators-10-tips**

Index